The Complete
MOM'S
Little Instruction Book

ANNIE PIGEON

Gramercy Books
New York

Originally published in two volumes by Pinnacle Books under the titles:

Mom's Little Instruction Book copyright © 1995 by Annie Pigeon
Mom's New Little Instruction Book copyright © 1995 by Annie Pigeon

This 2005 edition is published by Gramercy Books, an imprint of Random House Value Publishing, a division of Random House, Inc., New York, by arrangement with Kensington Publishing Corp.

Gramercy is a registered trademark and the colophon is a trademark of Random House, Inc.

Random House
New York • Toronto • London • Sydney • Auckland
www.randomhouse.com

Printed and bound in Singapore

Library of Congress Cataloging-in-Publication Data

Pigeon, Annie.
   The complete Mom's little instruction book : wit and wisdom for mothers / Annie Pigeon.
      p. cm.
   Originally published in two volumes under titles: Mom's little instruction book, and Mom's new little instruction book.
   New York : Pinnacle Books, c1995.
   ISBN 0-517-22325-2
   1. Motherhood—Miscellanea. I. Title.

HQ759.P533 2005
306.874'3—dc22
                                        2004052270

10 9 8 7 6 5 4 3 2 1

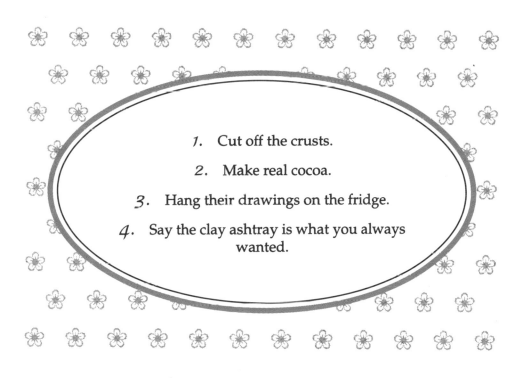

1. Cut off the crusts.

2. Make real cocoa.

3. Hang their drawings on the fridge.

4. Say the clay ashtray is what you always wanted.

5. Sing silly songs.

6. Make goofy faces.

7. Let them take off the training wheels.

8. Remind the Tooth Fairy about inflation.

9. Buy a good stain remover.

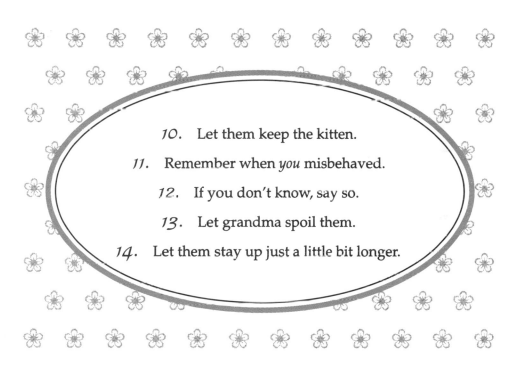

10. Let them keep the kitten.

11. Remember when *you* misbehaved.

12. If you don't know, say so.

13. Let grandma spoil them.

14. Let them stay up just a little bit longer.

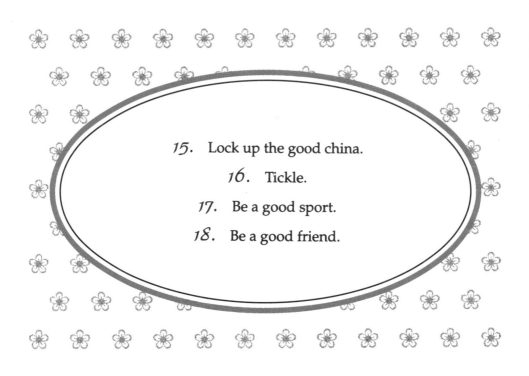

15. Lock up the good china.

16. Tickle.

17. Be a good sport.

18. Be a good friend.

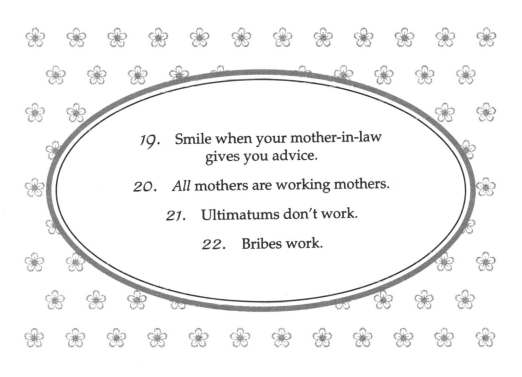

19. Smile when your mother-in-law gives you advice.

20. *All* mothers are working mothers.

21. Ultimatums don't work.

22. Bribes work.

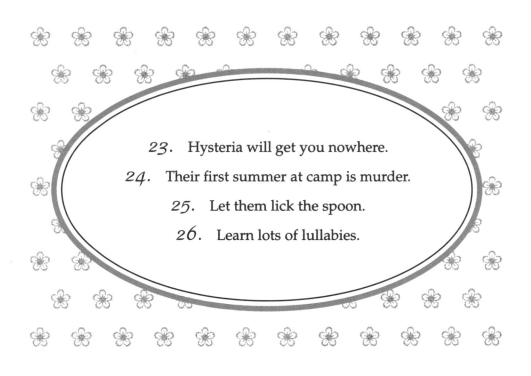

23. Hysteria will get you nowhere.

24. Their first summer at camp is murder.

25. Let them lick the spoon.

26. Learn lots of lullabies.

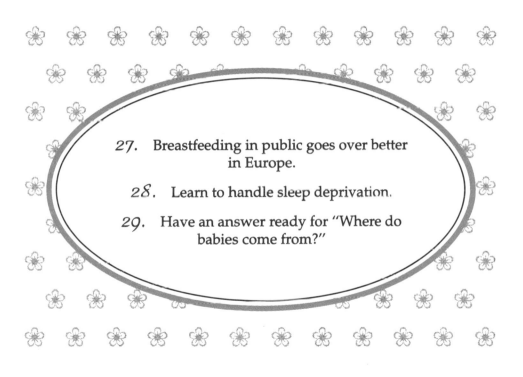

27. Breastfeeding in public goes over better in Europe.

28. Learn to handle sleep deprivation.

29. Have an answer ready for "Where do babies come from?"

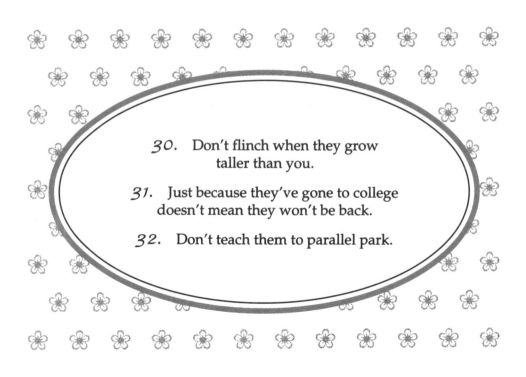

30. Don't flinch when they grow taller than you.

31. Just because they've gone to college doesn't mean they won't be back.

32. Don't teach them to parallel park.

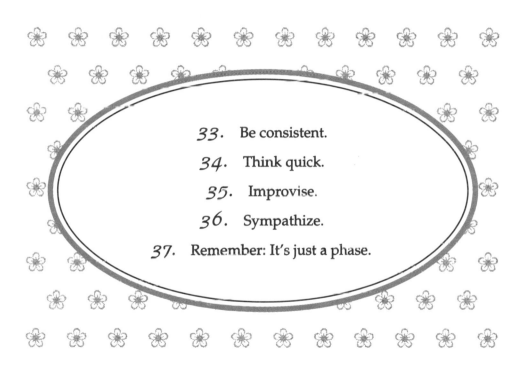

33. Be consistent.

34. Think quick.

35. Improvise.

36. Sympathize.

37. Remember: It's just a phase.

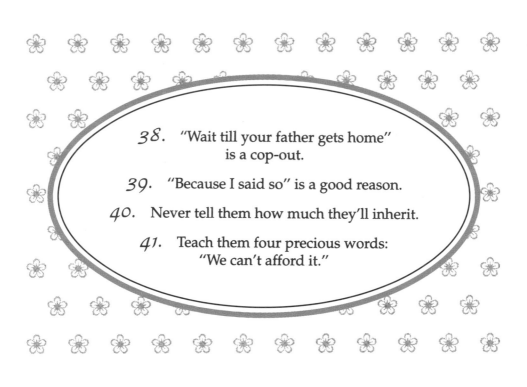

38. "Wait till your father gets home"
is a cop-out.

39. "Because I said so" is a good reason.

40. Never tell them how much they'll inherit.

41. Teach them four precious words:
"We can't afford it."

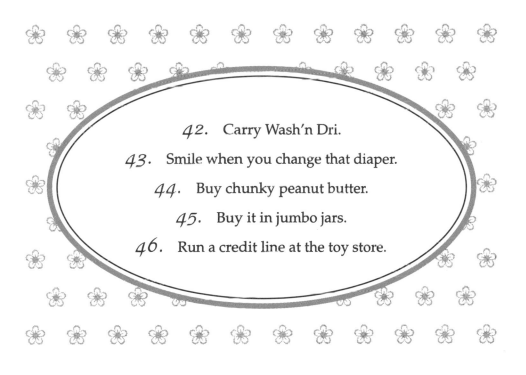

42. Carry Wash'n Dri.

43. Smile when you change that diaper.

44. Buy chunky peanut butter.

45. Buy it in jumbo jars.

46. Run a credit line at the toy store.

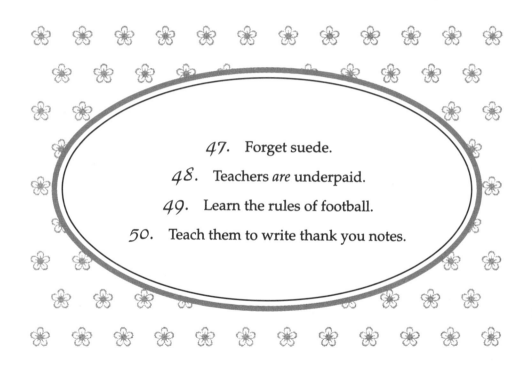

47. Forget suede.

48. Teachers *are* underpaid.

49. Learn the rules of football.

50. Teach them to write thank you notes.

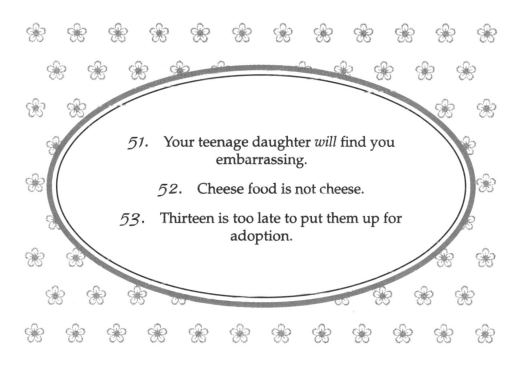

51. Your teenage daughter *will* find you embarrassing.

52. Cheese food is not cheese.

53. Thirteen is too late to put them up for adoption.

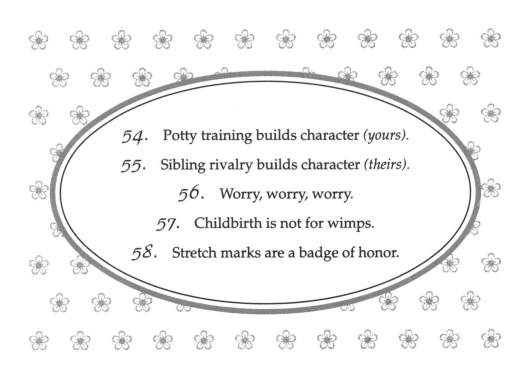

54. Potty training builds character *(yours)*.

55. Sibling rivalry builds character *(theirs)*.

56. Worry, worry, worry.

57. Childbirth is not for wimps.

58. Stretch marks are a badge of honor.

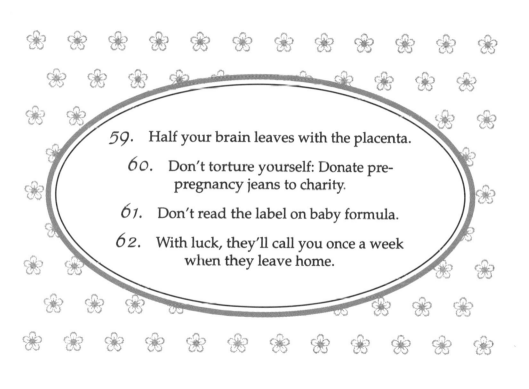

59. Half your brain leaves with the placenta.

60. Don't torture yourself: Donate pre-pregnancy jeans to charity.

61. Don't read the label on baby formula.

62. With luck, they'll call you once a week when they leave home.

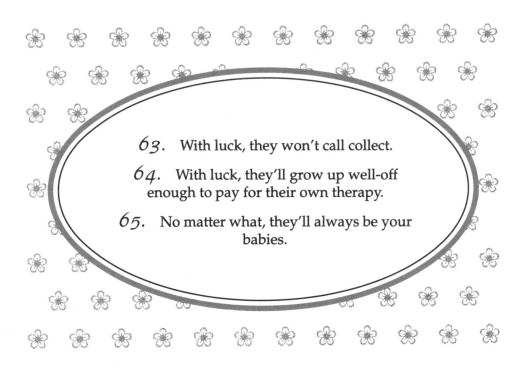

63. With luck, they won't call collect.

64. With luck, they'll grow up well-off enough to pay for their own therapy.

65. No matter what, they'll always be your babies.

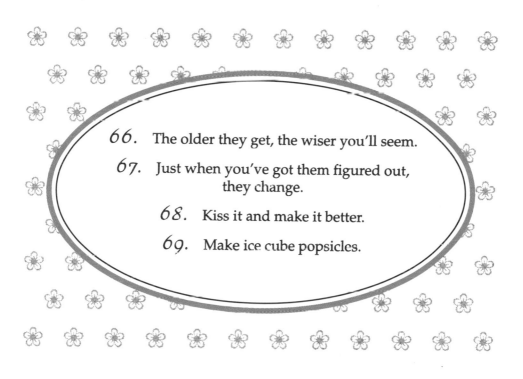

66. The older they get, the wiser you'll seem.

67. Just when you've got them figured out, they change.

68. Kiss it and make it better.

69. Make ice cube popsicles.

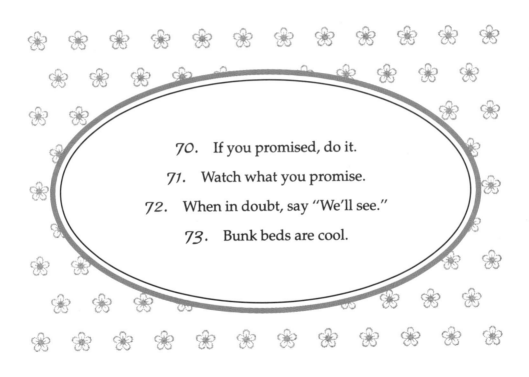

70. If you promised, do it.

71. Watch what you promise.

72. When in doubt, say "We'll see."

73. Bunk beds are cool.

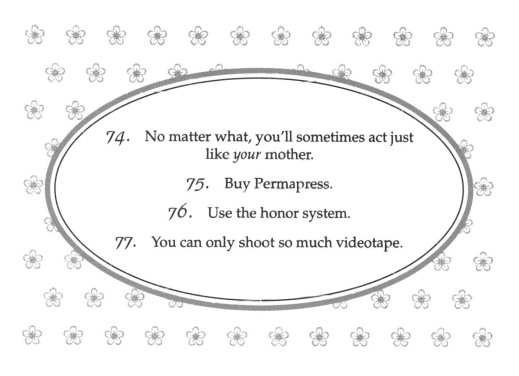

74. No matter what, you'll sometimes act just like *your* mother.

75. Buy Permapress.

76. Use the honor system.

77. You can only shoot so much videotape.

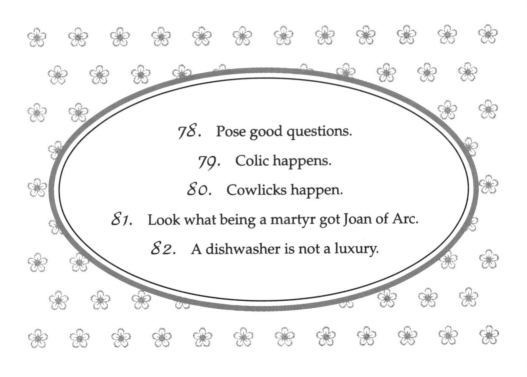

78. Pose good questions.

79. Colic happens.

80. Cowlicks happen.

81. Look what being a martyr got Joan of Arc.

82. A dishwasher is not a luxury.

83. The new math is harder than the old math.

84. Let's hear it for leftovers.

85. Don't leave their teddy bear behind.

86. Learn to make daisy chains.

87. Not everyone can be a valedictorian.

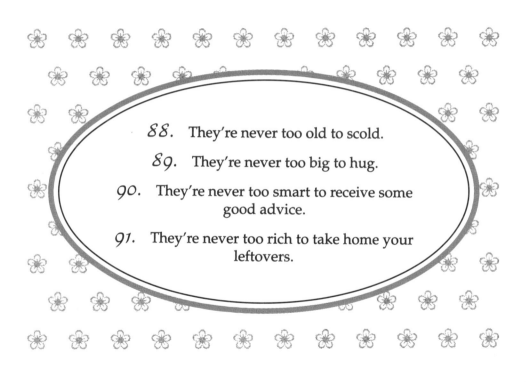

88. They're never too old to scold.

89. They're never too big to hug.

90. They're never too smart to receive some good advice.

91. They're never too rich to take home your leftovers.

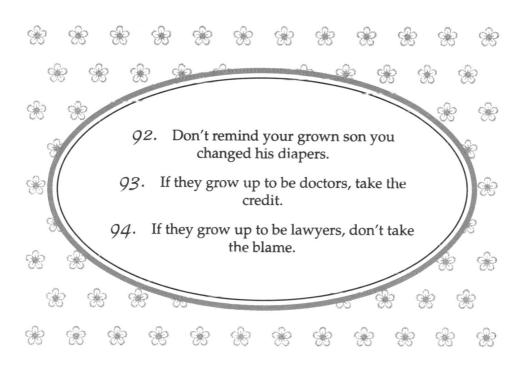

92. Don't remind your grown son you changed his diapers.

93. If they grow up to be doctors, take the credit.

94. If they grow up to be lawyers, don't take the blame.

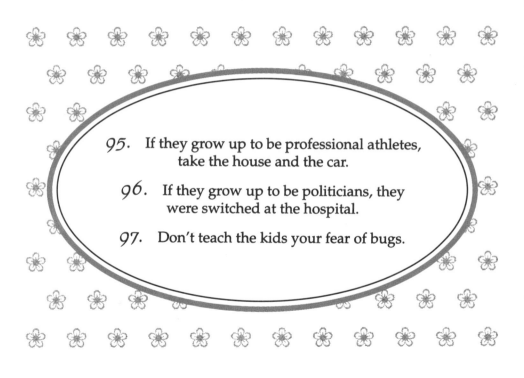

95. If they grow up to be professional athletes, take the house and the car.

96. If they grow up to be politicians, they were switched at the hospital.

97. Don't teach the kids your fear of bugs.

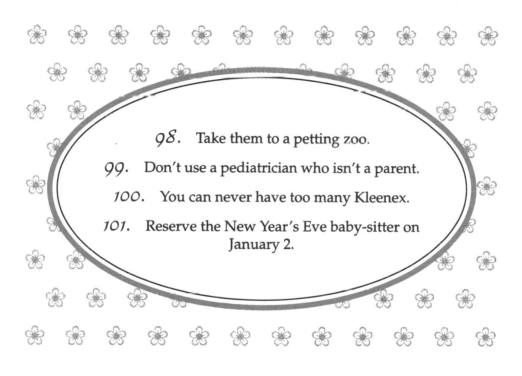

98. Take them to a petting zoo.

99. Don't use a pediatrician who isn't a parent.

100. You can never have too many Kleenex.

101. Reserve the New Year's Eve baby-sitter on January 2.

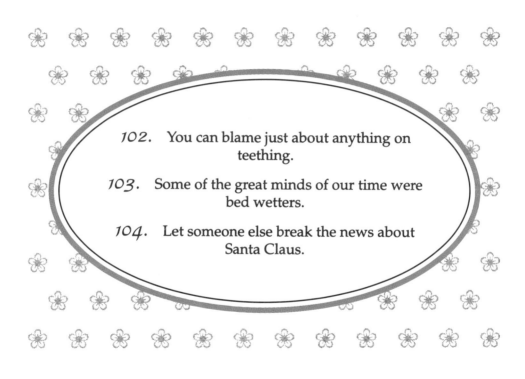

102. You can blame just about anything on teething.

103. Some of the great minds of our time were bed wetters.

104. Let someone else break the news about Santa Claus.

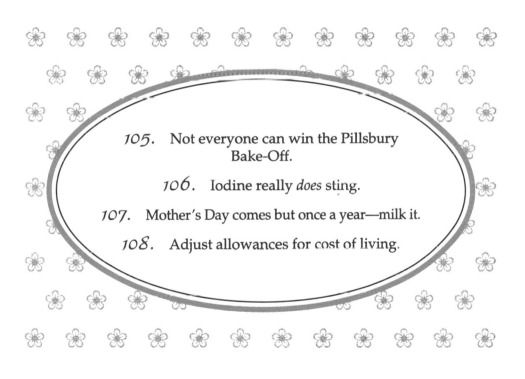

105. Not everyone can win the Pillsbury Bake-Off.

106. Iodine really *does* sting.

107. Mother's Day comes but once a year—milk it.

108. Adjust allowances for cost of living.

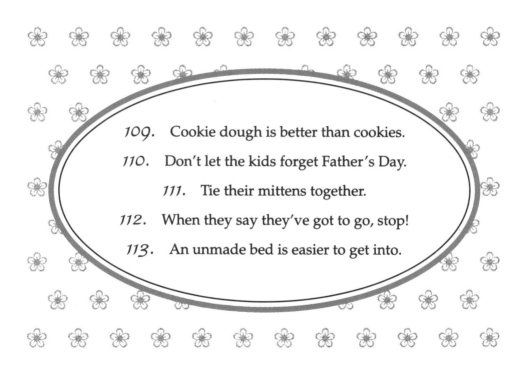

109. Cookie dough is better than cookies.

110. Don't let the kids forget Father's Day.

111. Tie their mittens together.

112. When they say they've got to go, stop!

113. An unmade bed is easier to get into.

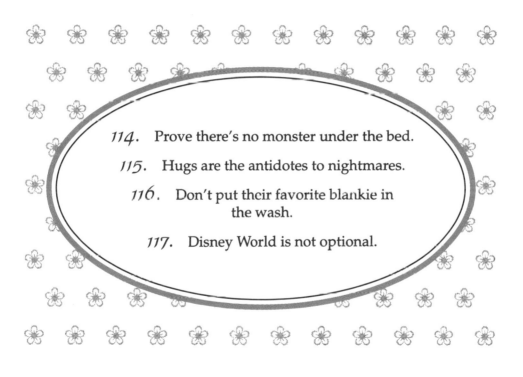

114. Prove there's no monster under the bed.

115. Hugs are the antidotes to nightmares.

116. Don't put their favorite blankie in the wash.

117. Disney World is not optional.

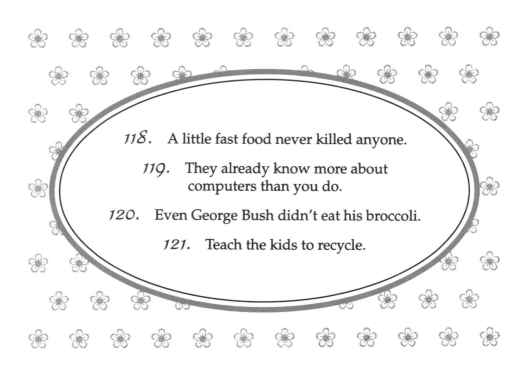

118. A little fast food never killed anyone.

119. They already know more about computers than you do.

120. Even George Bush didn't eat his broccoli.

121. Teach the kids to recycle.

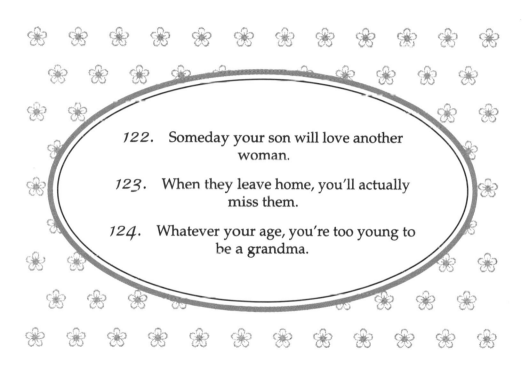

122. Someday your son will love another woman.

123. When they leave home, you'll actually miss them.

124. Whatever your age, you're too young to be a grandma.

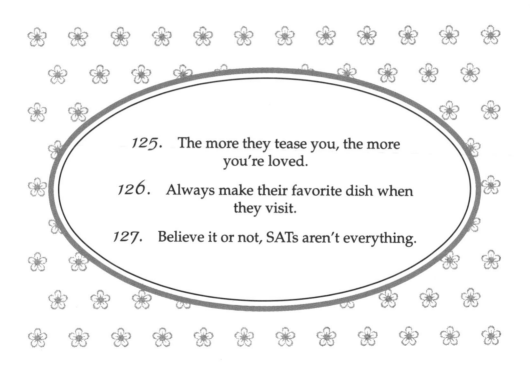

125. The more they tease you, the more you're loved.

126. Always make their favorite dish when they visit.

127. Believe it or not, SATs aren't everything.

128. Yes, it's important they wear what their friends wear.

129. Teenagers are *supposed* to dress goofy.

130. Yes, we're all tired of dinosaurs.

131. Anyone can make a secret special sauce.

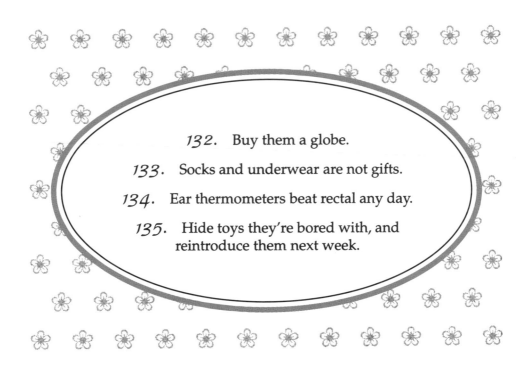

132. Buy them a globe.

133. Socks and underwear are not gifts.

134. Ear thermometers beat rectal any day.

135. Hide toys they're bored with, and reintroduce them next week.

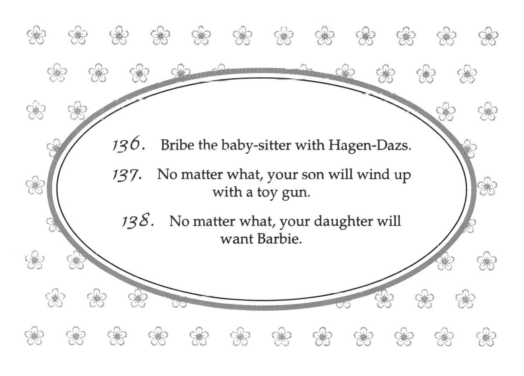

136. Bribe the baby-sitter with Hagen-Dazs.

137. No matter what, your son will wind up
with a toy gun.

138. No matter what, your daughter will
want Barbie.

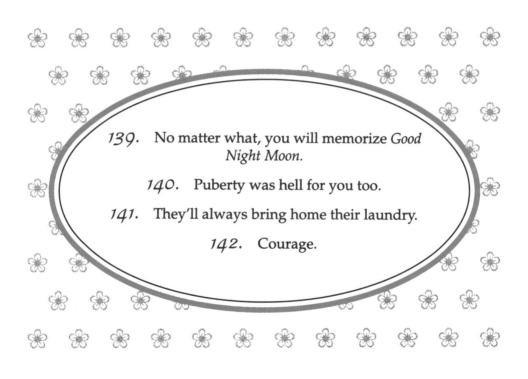

139. No matter what, you will memorize *Good Night Moon.*

140. Puberty was hell for you too.

141. They'll always bring home their laundry.

142. Courage.

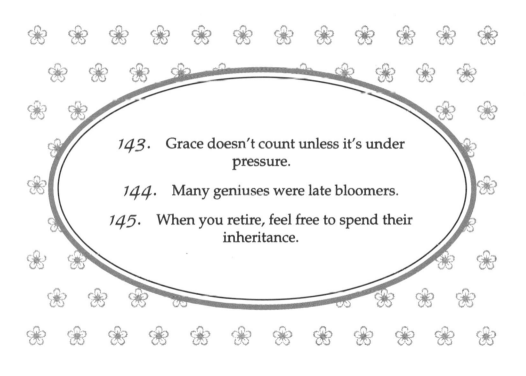

143. Grace doesn't count unless it's under pressure.

144. Many geniuses were late bloomers.

145. When you retire, feel free to spend their inheritance.

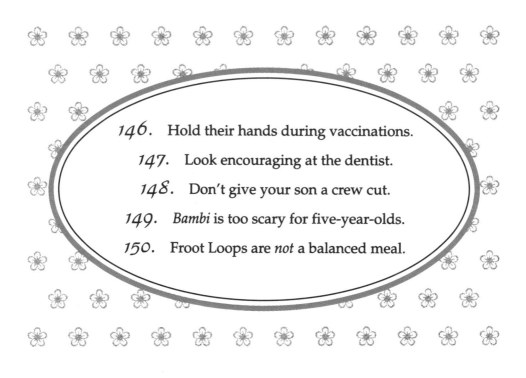

146. Hold their hands during vaccinations.

147. Look encouraging at the dentist.

148. Don't give your son a crew cut.

149. *Bambi* is too scary for five-year-olds.

150. Froot Loops are *not* a balanced meal.

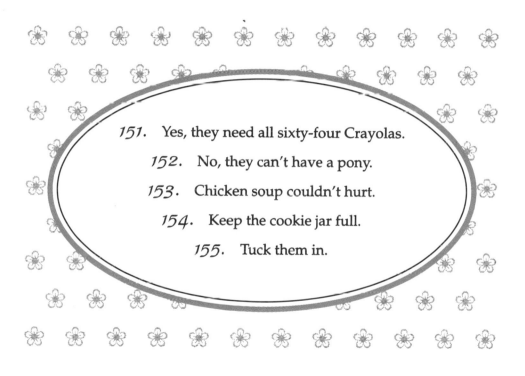

151. Yes, they need all sixty-four Crayolas.

152. No, they can't have a pony.

153. Chicken soup couldn't hurt.

154. Keep the cookie jar full.

155. Tuck them in.

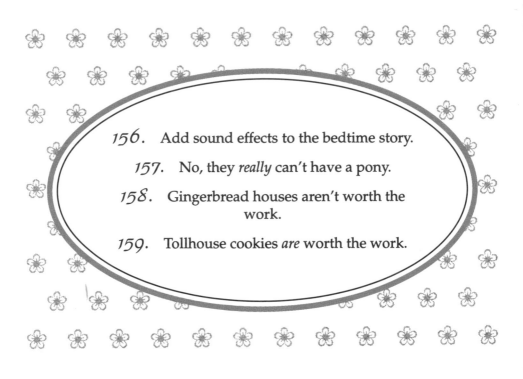

156. Add sound effects to the bedtime story.

157. No, they *really* can't have a pony.

158. Gingerbread houses aren't worth the work.

159. Tollhouse cookies *are* worth the work.

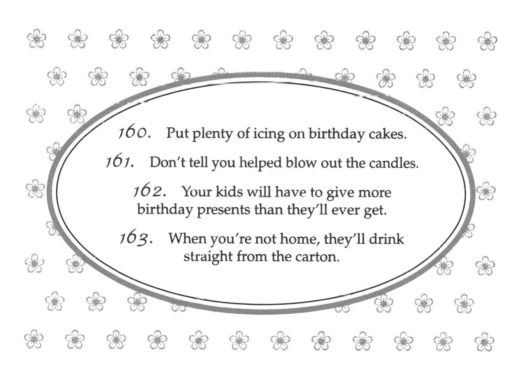

160. Put plenty of icing on birthday cakes.

161. Don't tell you helped blow out the candles.

162. Your kids will have to give more birthday presents than they'll ever get.

163. When you're not home, they'll drink straight from the carton.

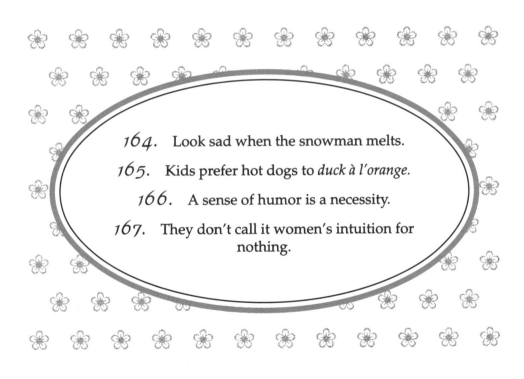

164. Look sad when the snowman melts.

165. Kids prefer hot dogs to *duck à l'orange*.

166. A sense of humor is a necessity.

167. They don't call it women's intuition for nothing.

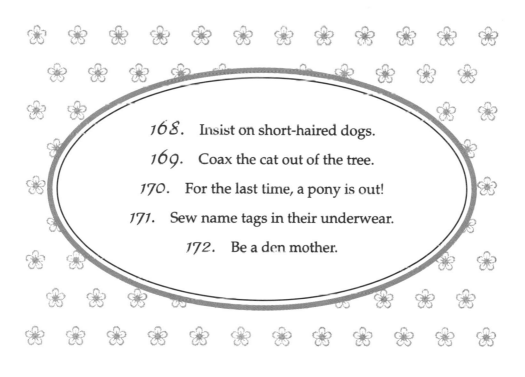

168. Insist on short-haired dogs.

169. Coax the cat out of the tree.

170. For the last time, a pony is out!

171. Sew name tags in their underwear.

172. Be a den mother.

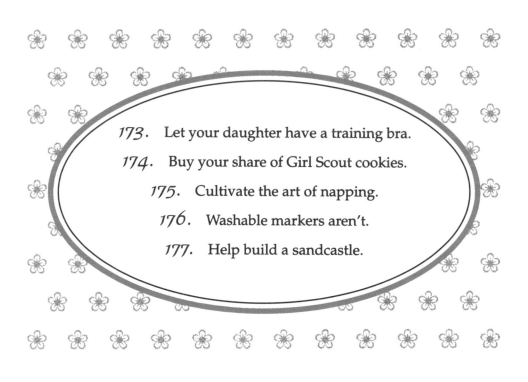

173. Let your daughter have a training bra.

174. Buy your share of Girl Scout cookies.

175. Cultivate the art of napping.

176. Washable markers aren't.

177. Help build a sandcastle.

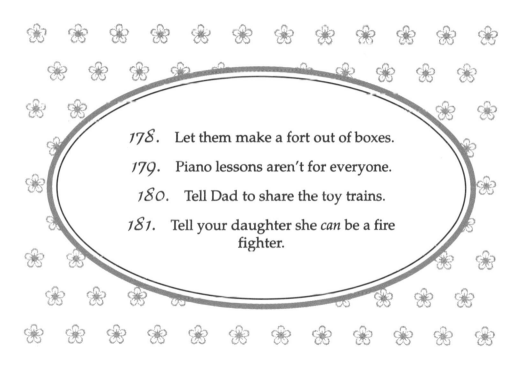

178. Let them make a fort out of boxes.

179. Piano lessons aren't for everyone.

180. Tell Dad to share the toy trains.

181. Tell your daughter she *can* be a fire fighter.

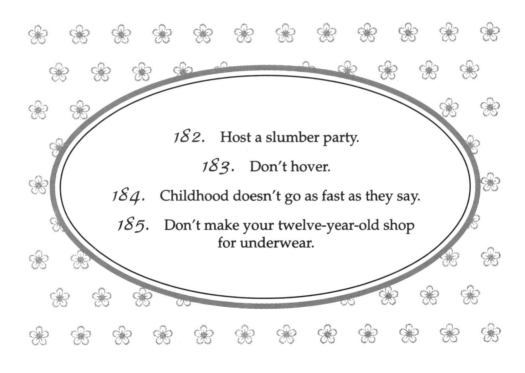

182. Host a slumber party.

183. Don't hover.

184. Childhood doesn't go as fast as they say.

185. Don't make your twelve-year-old shop for underwear.

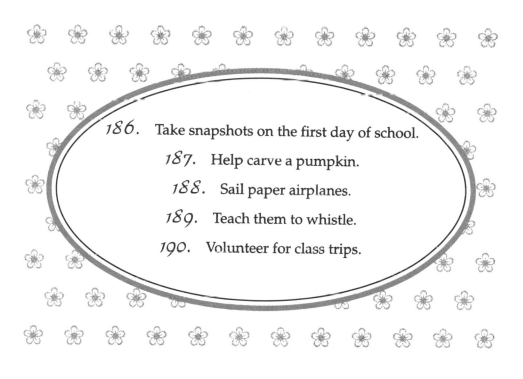

186. Take snapshots on the first day of school.

187. Help carve a pumpkin.

188. Sail paper airplanes.

189. Teach them to whistle.

190. Volunteer for class trips.

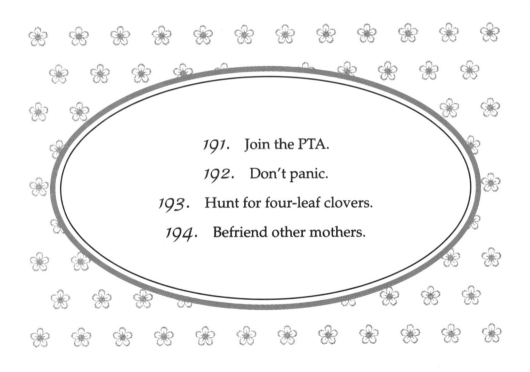

191. Join the PTA.

192. Don't panic.

193. Hunt for four-leaf clovers.

194. Befriend other mothers.

195. Don't let your kids record your answering machine message.

196. Scotchguard everything.

197. There's a little Martha Stewart in all of us.

198. Never use the check-out with the candy display.

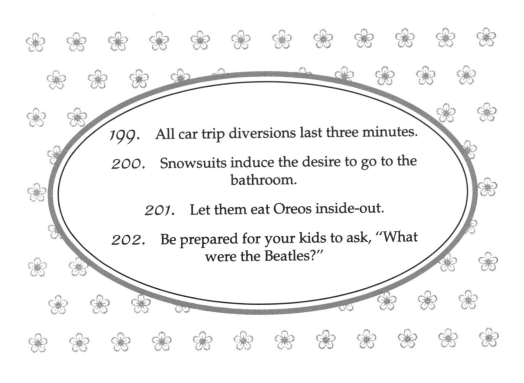

199. All car trip diversions last three minutes.

200. Snowsuits induce the desire to go to the bathroom.

201. Let them eat Oreos inside-out.

202. Be prepared for your kids to ask, "What were the Beatles?"

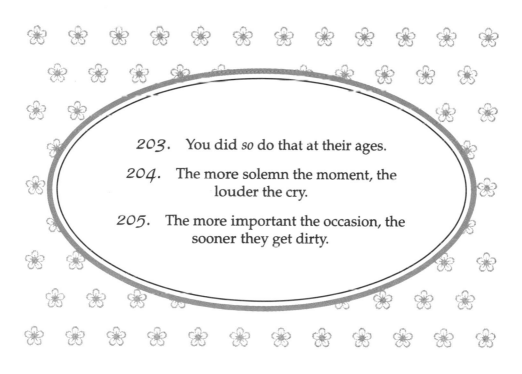

203. You did *so* do that at their ages.

204. The more solemn the moment, the louder the cry.

205. The more important the occasion, the sooner they get dirty.

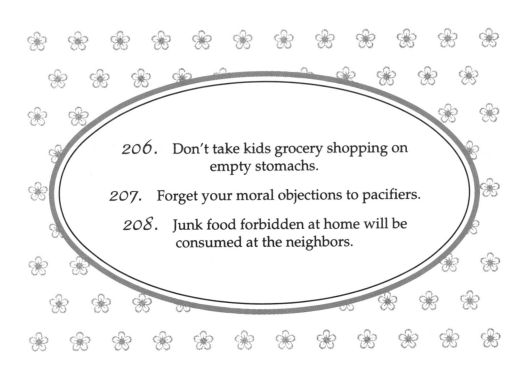

206. Don't take kids grocery shopping on empty stomachs.

207. Forget your moral objections to pacifiers.

208. Junk food forbidden at home will be consumed at the neighbors.

209. TV shows prohibited at home will be watched at the neighbors.

210. Tell know-it-alls: Mind your own business.

211. Put a lock on your bedroom door.

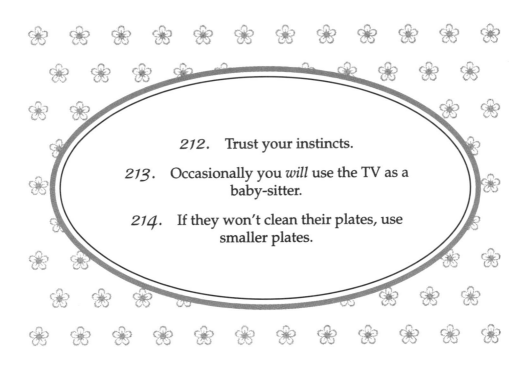

212. Trust your instincts.

213. Occasionally you *will* use the TV as a baby-sitter.

214. If they won't clean their plates, use smaller plates.

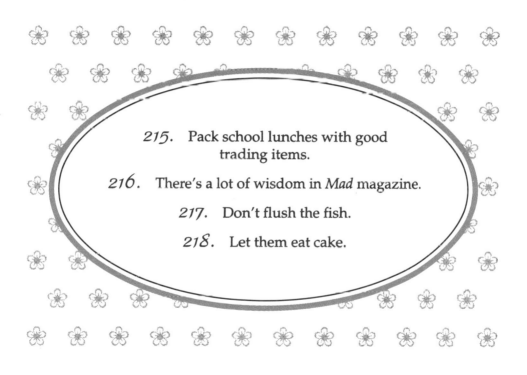

215. Pack school lunches with good trading items.

216. There's a lot of wisdom in *Mad* magazine.

217. Don't flush the fish.

218. Let them eat cake.

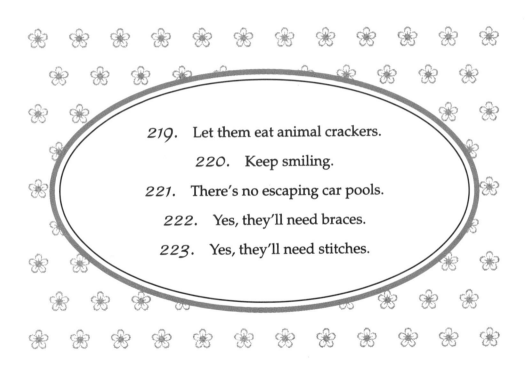

219. Let them eat animal crackers.

220. Keep smiling.

221. There's no escaping car pools.

222. Yes, they'll need braces.

223. Yes, they'll need stitches.

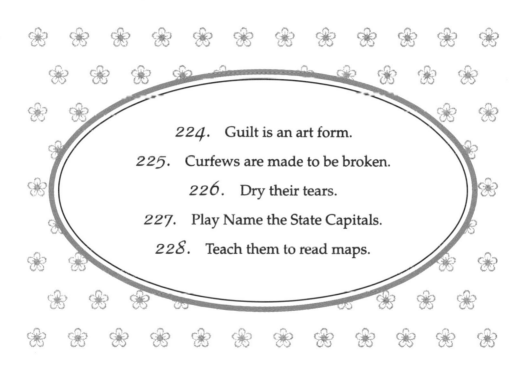

224. Guilt is an art form.

225. Curfews are made to be broken.

226. Dry their tears.

227. Play Name the State Capitals.

228. Teach them to read maps.

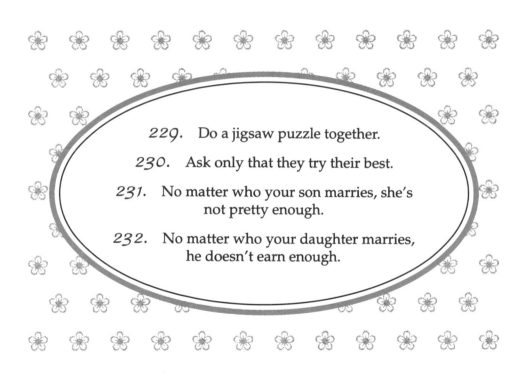

229.   Do a jigsaw puzzle together.

230.   Ask only that they try their best.

231.   No matter who your son marries, she's not pretty enough.

232.   No matter who your daughter marries, he doesn't earn enough.

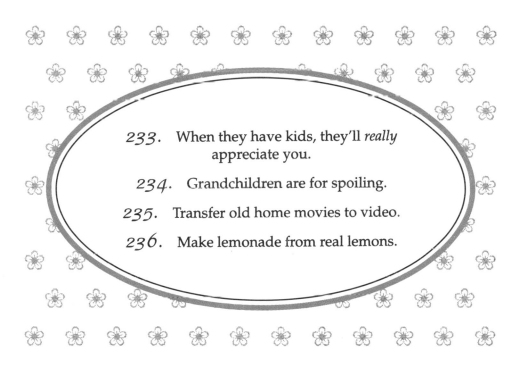

233. When they have kids, they'll *really* appreciate you.

234. Grandchildren are for spoiling.

235. Transfer old home movies to video.

236. Make lemonade from real lemons.

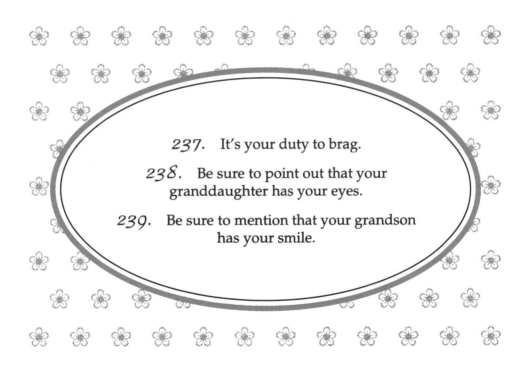

237. It's your duty to brag.

238. Be sure to point out that your granddaughter has your eyes.

239. Be sure to mention that your grandson has your smile.

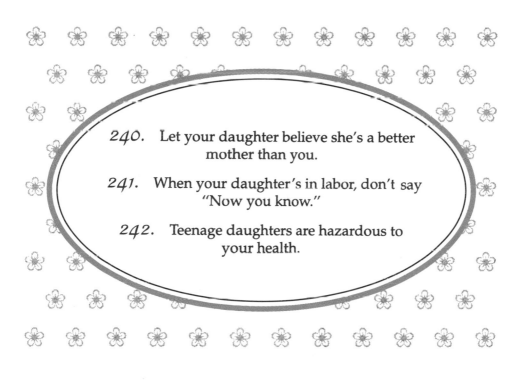

240. Let your daughter believe she's a better mother than you.

241. When your daughter's in labor, don't say "Now you know."

242. Teenage daughters are hazardous to your health.

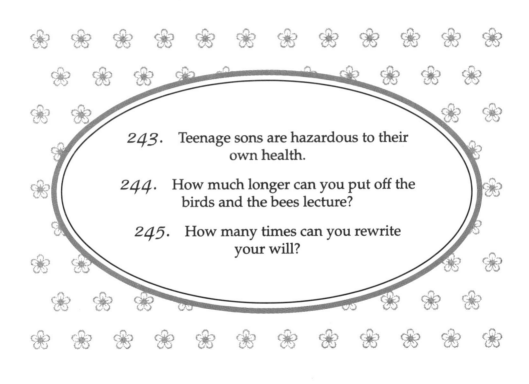

243. Teenage sons are hazardous to their own health.

244. How much longer can you put off the birds and the bees lecture?

245. How many times can you rewrite your will?

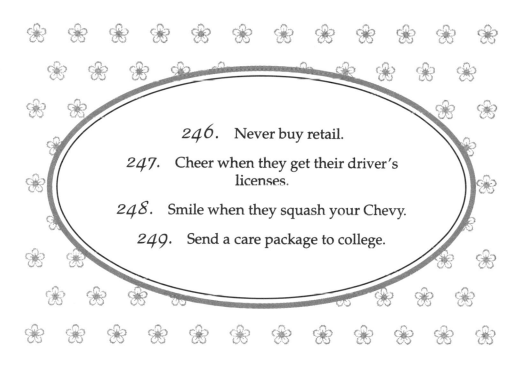

246. Never buy retail.

247. Cheer when they get their driver's licenses.

248. Smile when they squash your Chevy.

249. Send a care package to college.

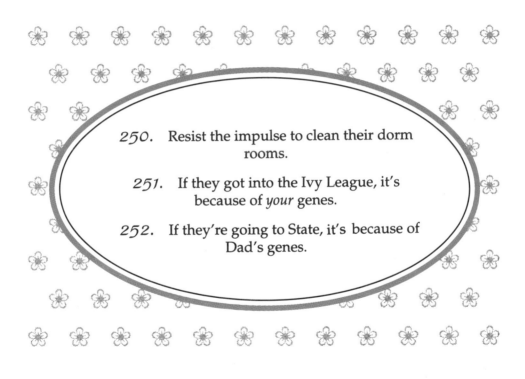

250. Resist the impulse to clean their dorm rooms.

251. If they got into the Ivy League, it's because of *your* genes.

252. If they're going to State, it's because of Dad's genes.

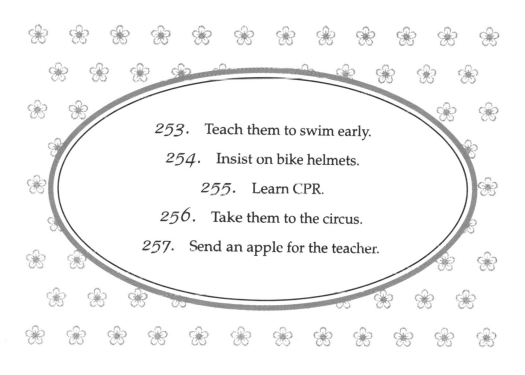

253. Teach them to swim early.

254. Insist on bike helmets.

255. Learn CPR.

256. Take them to the circus.

257. Send an apple for the teacher.

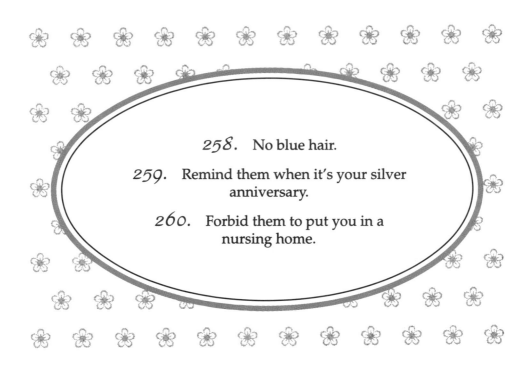

258. No blue hair.

259. Remind them when it's your silver anniversary.

260. Forbid them to put you in a nursing home.

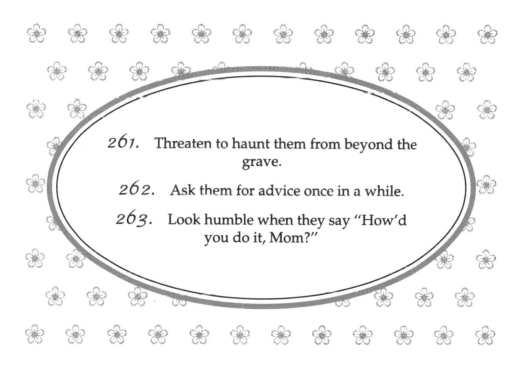

261. Threaten to haunt them from beyond the grave.

262. Ask them for advice once in a while.

263. Look humble when they say "How'd you do it, Mom?"

264. Pass along your wedding dress to your daughter.

265. Give Snickers at Halloween.

266. Remember the names of their stuffed animals.

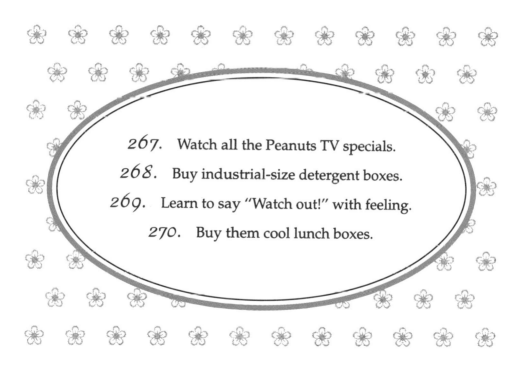

267. Watch all the Peanuts TV specials.

268. Buy industrial-size detergent boxes.

269. Learn to say "Watch out!" with feeling.

270. Buy them cool lunch boxes.

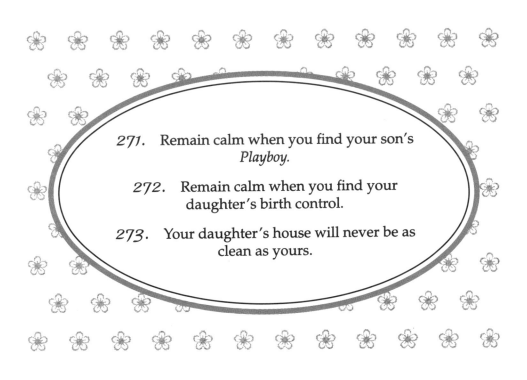

271. Remain calm when you find your son's *Playboy*.

272. Remain calm when you find your daughter's birth control.

273. Your daughter's house will never be as clean as yours.

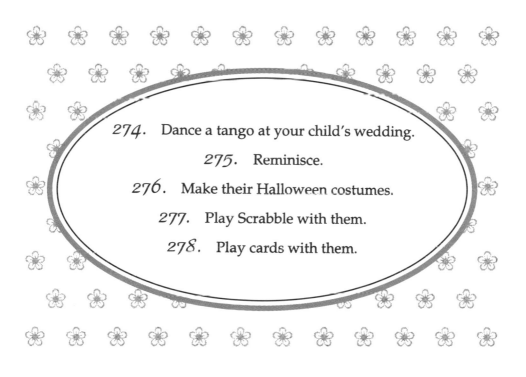

274. Dance a tango at your child's wedding.

275. Reminisce.

276. Make their Halloween costumes.

277. Play Scrabble with them.

278. Play cards with them.

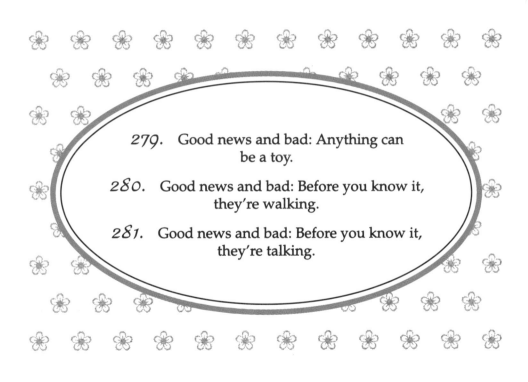

279. Good news and bad: Anything can be a toy.

280. Good news and bad: Before you know it, they're walking.

281. Good news and bad: Before you know it, they're talking.

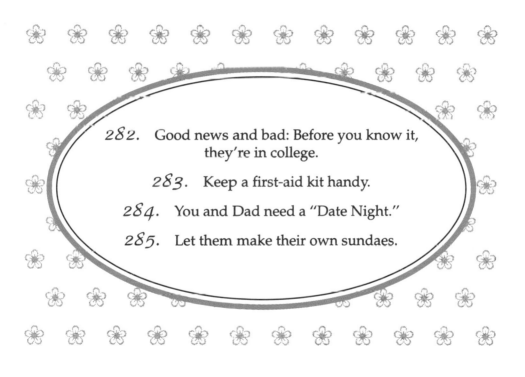

282. Good news and bad: Before you know it,
they're in college.

283. Keep a first-aid kit handy.

284. You and Dad need a "Date Night."

285. Let them make their own sundaes.

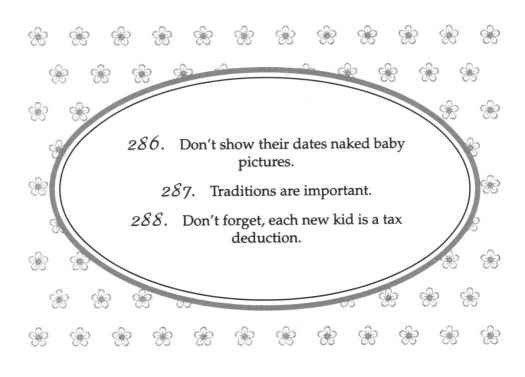

286. Don't show their dates naked baby pictures.

287. Traditions are important.

288. Don't forget, each new kid is a tax deduction.

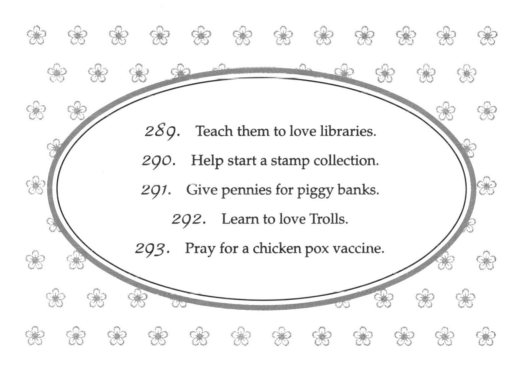

289. Teach them to love libraries.

290. Help start a stamp collection.

291. Give pennies for piggy banks.

292. Learn to love Trolls.

293. Pray for a chicken pox vaccine.

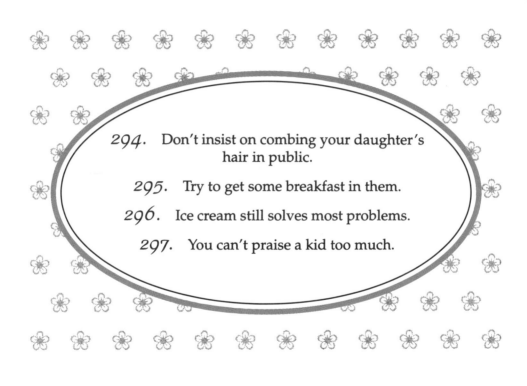

294. Don't insist on combing your daughter's hair in public.

295. Try to get some breakfast in them.

296. Ice cream still solves most problems.

297. You can't praise a kid too much.

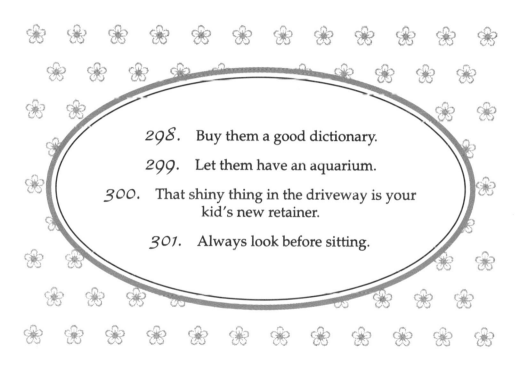

298. Buy them a good dictionary.

299. Let them have an aquarium.

300. That shiny thing in the driveway is your kid's new retainer.

301. Always look before sitting.

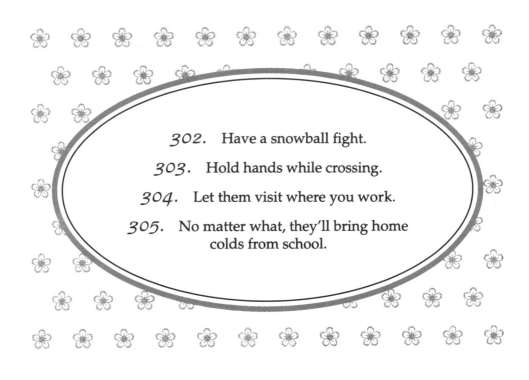

302. Have a snowball fight.

303. Hold hands while crossing.

304. Let them visit where you work.

305. No matter what, they'll bring home
colds from school.

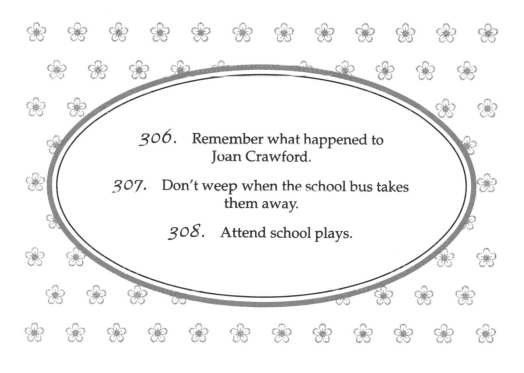

306. Remember what happened to
Joan Crawford.

307. Don't weep when the school bus takes
them away.

308. Attend school plays.

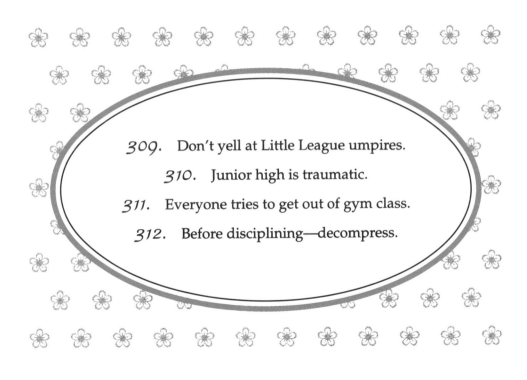

309. Don't yell at Little League umpires.

310. Junior high is traumatic.

311. Everyone tries to get out of gym class.

312. Before disciplining—decompress.

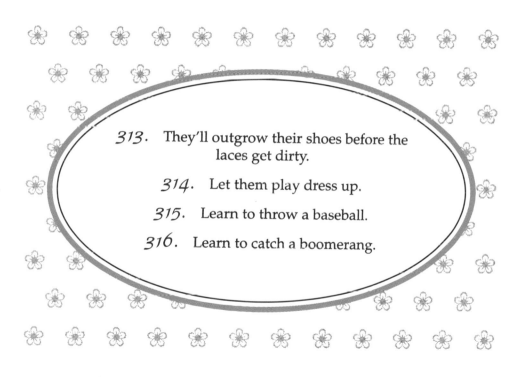

313. They'll outgrow their shoes before the laces get dirty.

314. Let them play dress up.

315. Learn to throw a baseball.

316. Learn to catch a boomerang.

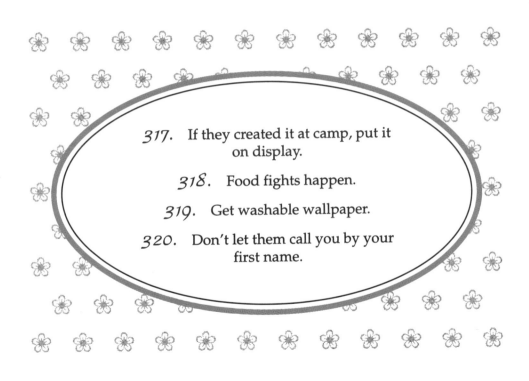

317. If they created it at camp, put it on display.

318. Food fights happen.

319. Get washable wallpaper.

320. Don't let them call you by your first name.

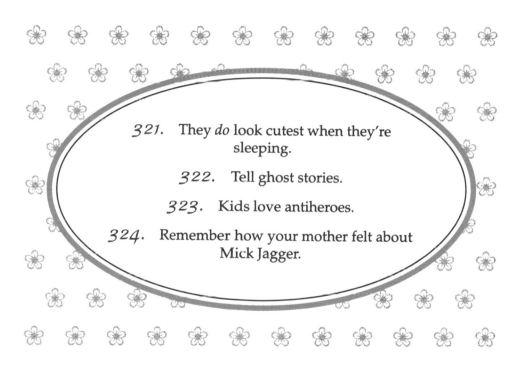

321. They *do* look cutest when they're sleeping.

322. Tell ghost stories.

323. Kids love antiheroes.

324. Remember how your mother felt about Mick Jagger.

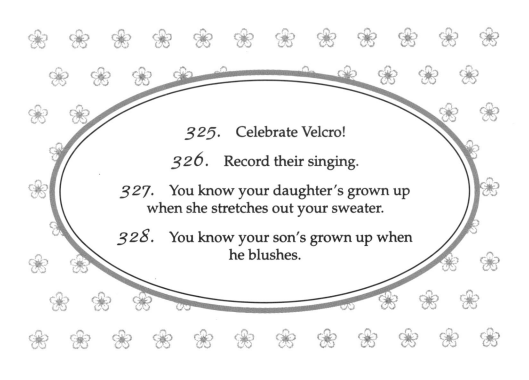

325. Celebrate Velcro!

326. Record their singing.

327. You know your daughter's grown up when she stretches out your sweater.

328. You know your son's grown up when he blushes.

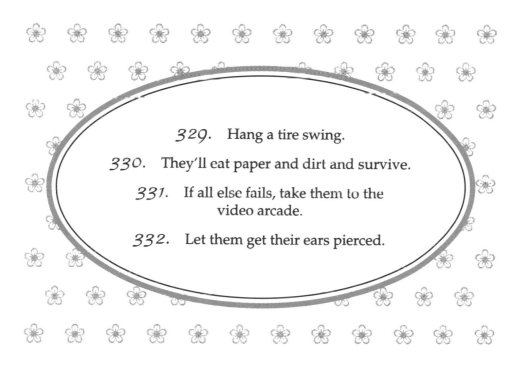

329. Hang a tire swing.

330. They'll eat paper and dirt and survive.

331. If all else fails, take them to the video arcade.

332. Let them get their ears pierced.

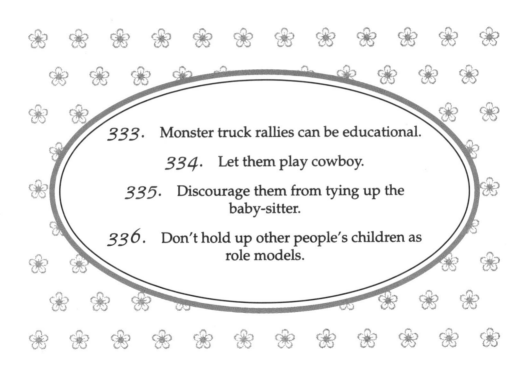

333. Monster truck rallies can be educational.

334. Let them play cowboy.

335. Discourage them from tying up the baby-sitter.

336. Don't hold up other people's children as role models.

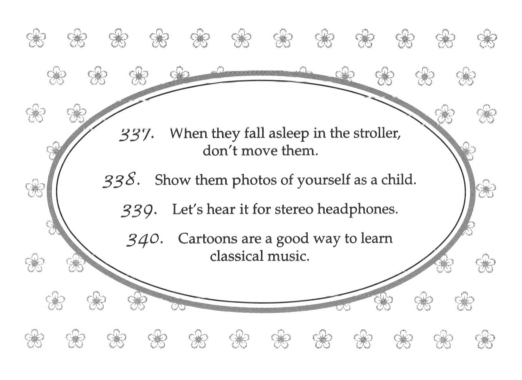

337. When they fall asleep in the stroller, don't move them.

338. Show them photos of yourself as a child.

339. Let's hear it for stereo headphones.

340. Cartoons are a good way to learn classical music.

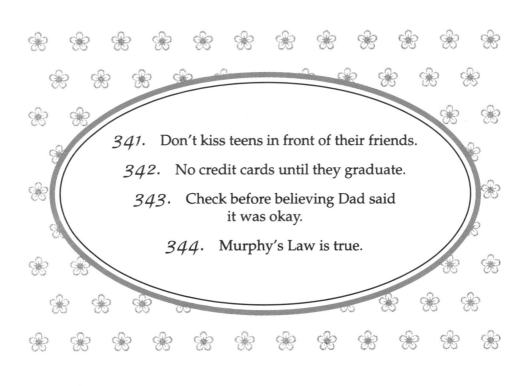

341. Don't kiss teens in front of their friends.

342. No credit cards until they graduate.

343. Check before believing Dad said
it was okay.

344. Murphy's Law is true.

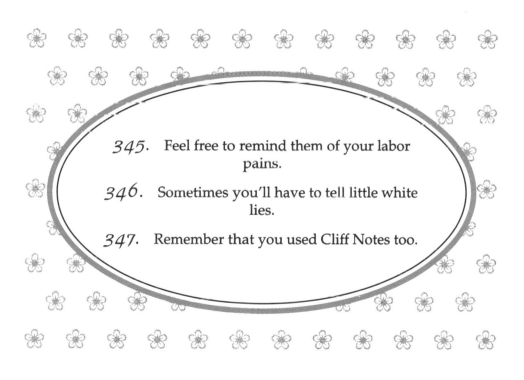

345. Feel free to remind them of your labor pains.

346. Sometimes you'll have to tell little white lies.

347. Remember that you used Cliff Notes too.

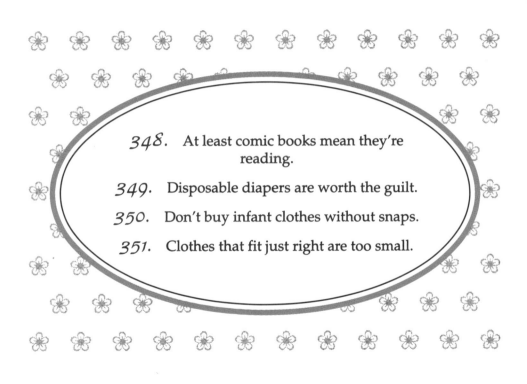

348. At least comic books mean they're reading.

349. Disposable diapers are worth the guilt.

350. Don't buy infant clothes without snaps.

351. Clothes that fit just right are too small.

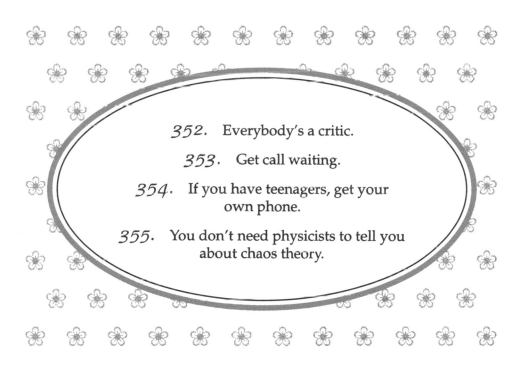

352. Everybody's a critic.

353. Get call waiting.

354. If you have teenagers, get your own phone.

355. You don't need physicists to tell you about chaos theory.

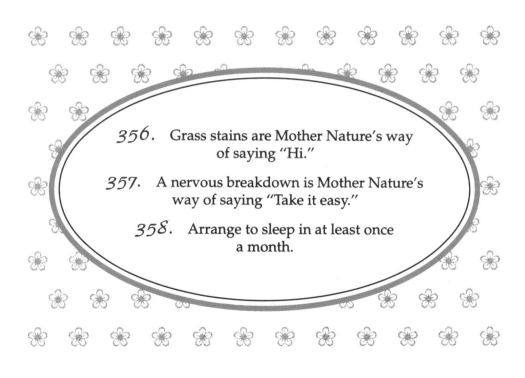

356. Grass stains are Mother Nature's way of saying "Hi."

357. A nervous breakdown is Mother Nature's way of saying "Take it easy."

358. Arrange to sleep in at least once a month.

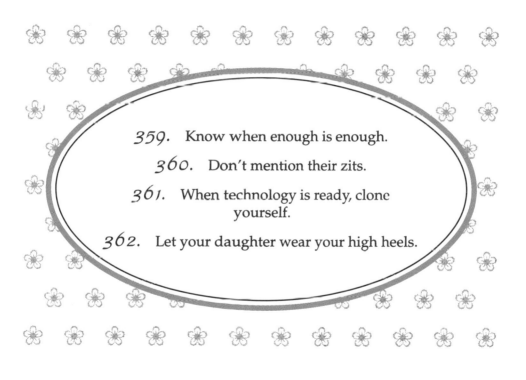

359. Know when enough is enough.

360. Don't mention their zits.

361. When technology is ready, clone yourself.

362. Let your daughter wear your high heels.

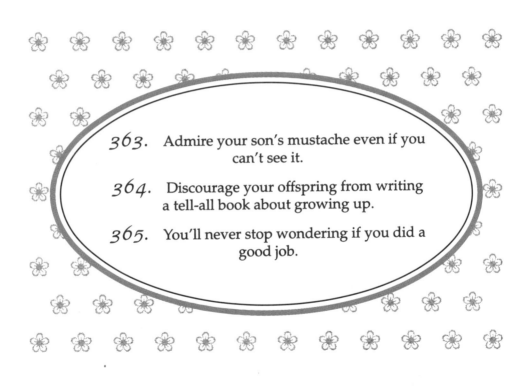

363. Admire your son's mustache even if you can't see it.

364. Discourage your offspring from writing a tell-all book about growing up.

365. You'll never stop wondering if you did a good job.

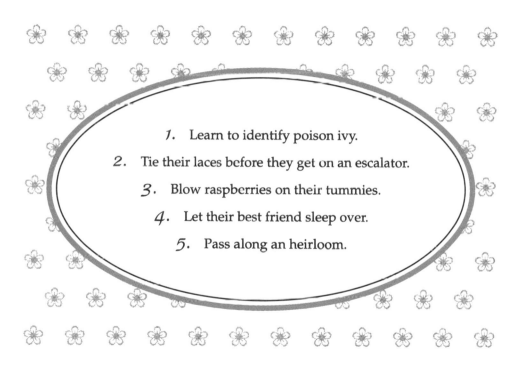

1. Learn to identify poison ivy.

2. Tie their laces before they get on an escalator.

3. Blow raspberries on their tummies.

4. Let their best friend sleep over.

5. Pass along an heirloom.

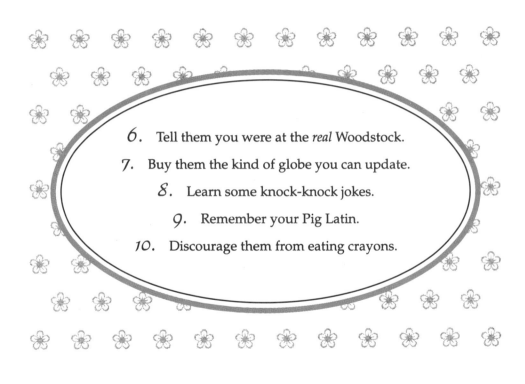

6. Tell them you were at the *real* Woodstock.

7. Buy them the kind of globe you can update.

8. Learn some knock-knock jokes.

9. Remember your Pig Latin.

10. Discourage them from eating crayons.

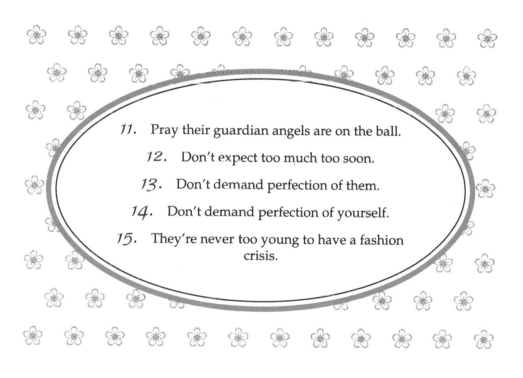

11. Pray their guardian angels are on the ball.

12. Don't expect too much too soon.

13. Don't demand perfection of them.

14. Don't demand perfection of yourself.

15. They're never too young to have a fashion crisis.

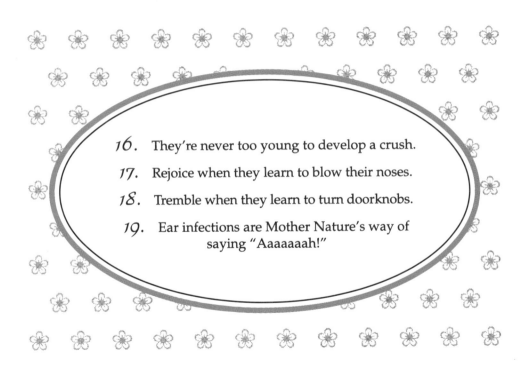

16. They're never too young to develop a crush.

17. Rejoice when they learn to blow their noses.

18. Tremble when they learn to turn doorknobs.

19. Ear infections are Mother Nature's way of saying "Aaaaaaah!"

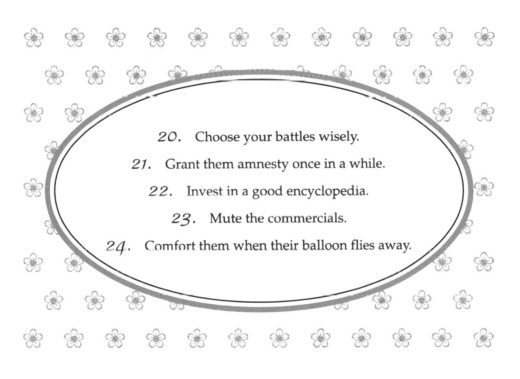

20. Choose your battles wisely.

21. Grant them amnesty once in a while.

22. Invest in a good encyclopedia.

23. Mute the commercials.

24. Comfort them when their balloon flies away.

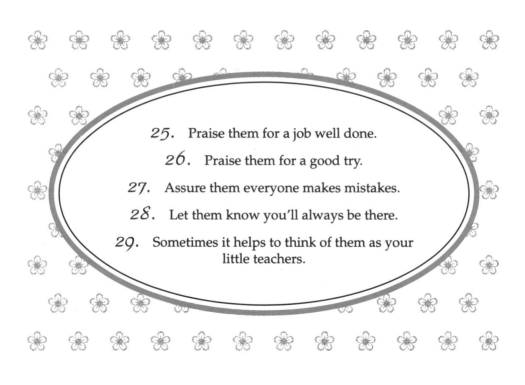

25. Praise them for a job well done.

26. Praise them for a good try.

27. Assure them everyone makes mistakes.

28. Let them know you'll always be there.

29. Sometimes it helps to think of them as your little teachers.

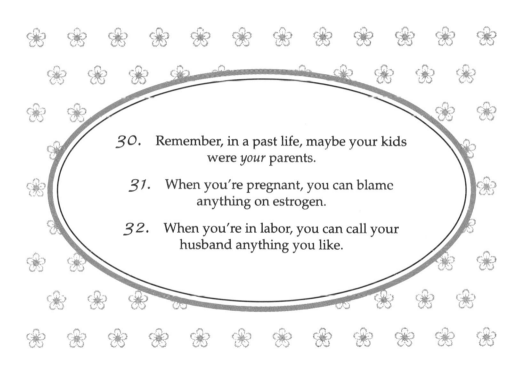

30. Remember, in a past life, maybe your kids were *your* parents.

31. When you're pregnant, you can blame anything on estrogen.

32. When you're in labor, you can call your husband anything you like.

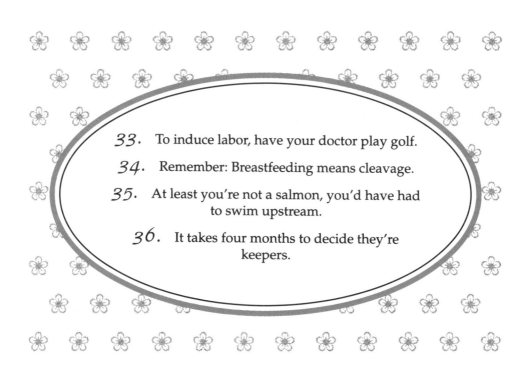

33. To induce labor, have your doctor play golf.

34. Remember: Breastfeeding means cleavage.

35. At least you're not a salmon, you'd have had to swim upstream.

36. It takes four months to decide they're keepers.

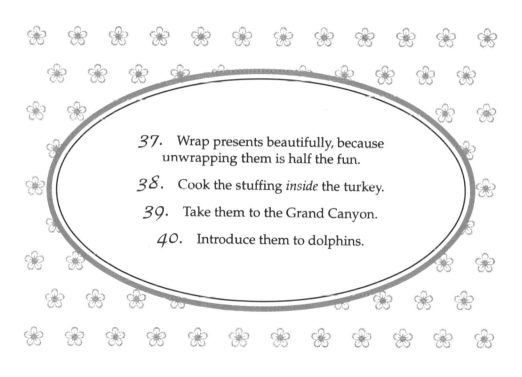

37. Wrap presents beautifully, because unwrapping them is half the fun.

38. Cook the stuffing *inside* the turkey.

39. Take them to the Grand Canyon.

40. Introduce them to dolphins.

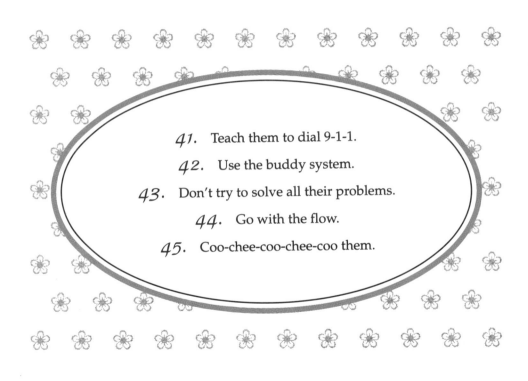

41. Teach them to dial 9-1-1.

42. Use the buddy system.

43. Don't try to solve all their problems.

44. Go with the flow.

45. Coo-chee-coo-chee-coo them.

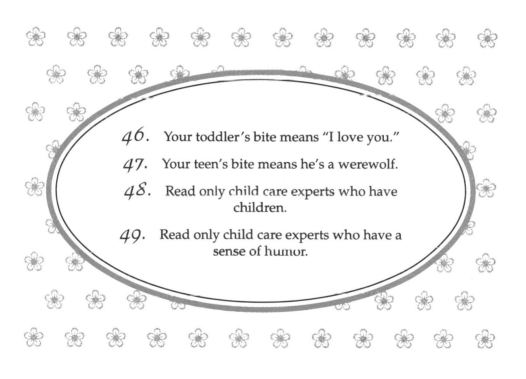

46. Your toddler's bite means "I love you."

47. Your teen's bite means he's a werewolf.

48. Read only child care experts who have children.

49. Read only child care experts who have a sense of humor.

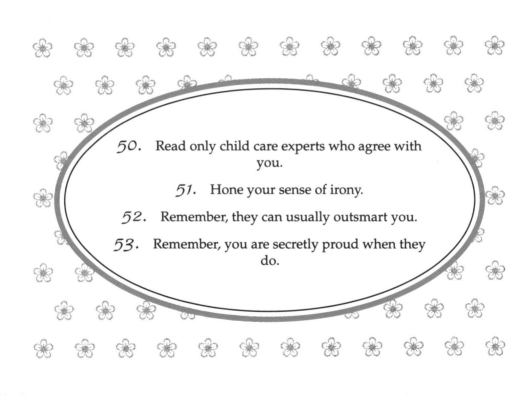

50. Read only child care experts who agree with you.

51. Hone your sense of irony.

52. Remember, they can usually outsmart you.

53. Remember, you are secretly proud when they do.

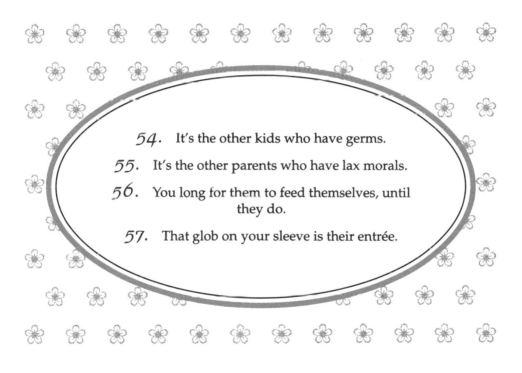

54. It's the other kids who have germs.

55. It's the other parents who have lax morals.

56. You long for them to feed themselves, until they do.

57. That glob on your sleeve is their entrée.

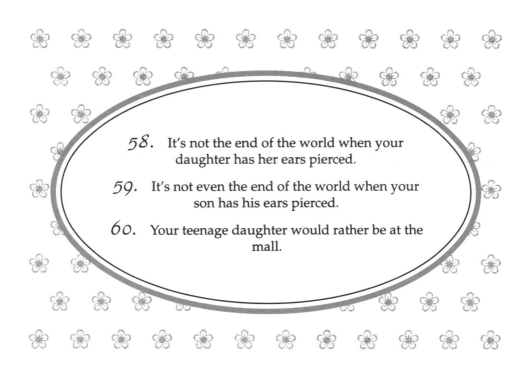

58. It's not the end of the world when your daughter has her ears pierced.

59. It's not even the end of the world when your son has his ears pierced.

60. Your teenage daughter would rather be at the mall.

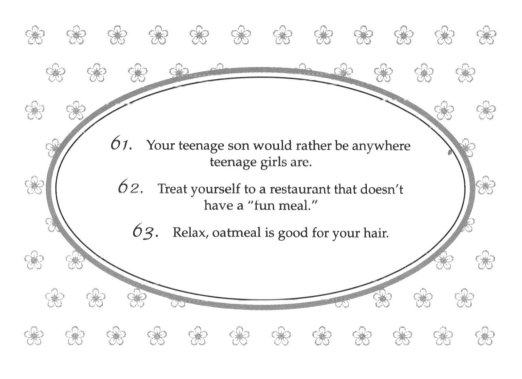

61. Your teenage son would rather be anywhere teenage girls are.

62. Treat yourself to a restaurant that doesn't have a "fun meal."

63. Relax, oatmeal is good for your hair.

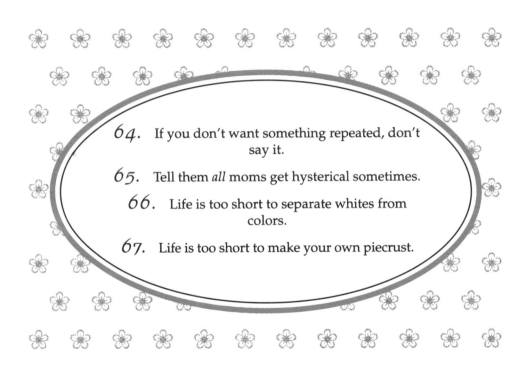

64. If you don't want something repeated, don't say it.

65. Tell them *all* moms get hysterical sometimes.

66. Life is too short to separate whites from colors.

67. Life is too short to make your own piecrust.

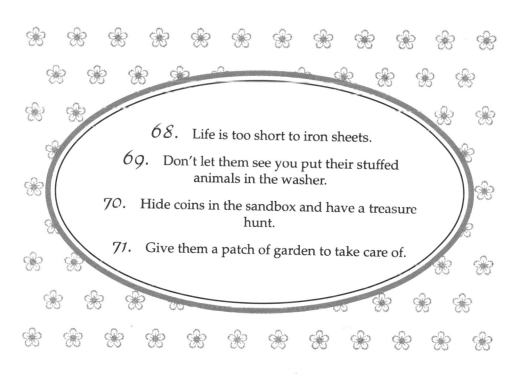

68. Life is too short to iron sheets.

69. Don't let them see you put their stuffed animals in the washer.

70. Hide coins in the sandbox and have a treasure hunt.

71. Give them a patch of garden to take care of.

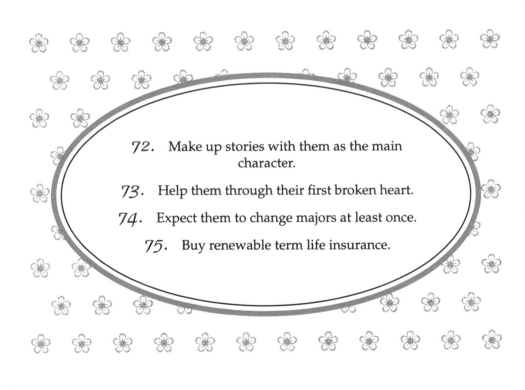

72. Make up stories with them as the main character.

73. Help them through their first broken heart.

74. Expect them to change majors at least once.

75. Buy renewable term life insurance.

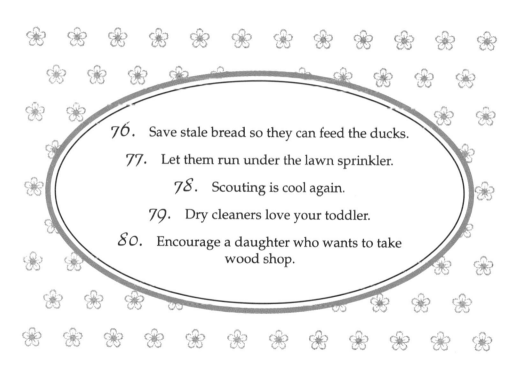

76. Save stale bread so they can feed the ducks.

77. Let them run under the lawn sprinkler.

78. Scouting is cool again.

79. Dry cleaners love your toddler.

80. Encourage a daughter who wants to take wood shop.

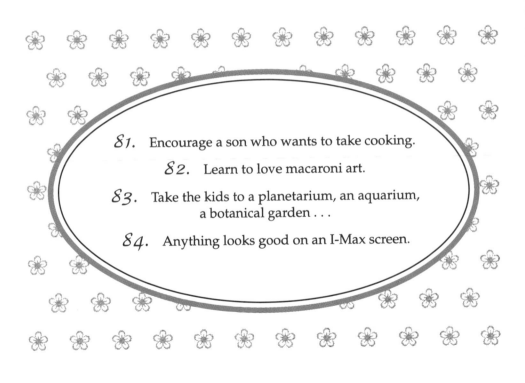

81. Encourage a son who wants to take cooking.

82. Learn to love macaroni art.

83. Take the kids to a planetarium, an aquarium, a botanical garden . . .

84. Anything looks good on an I-Max screen.

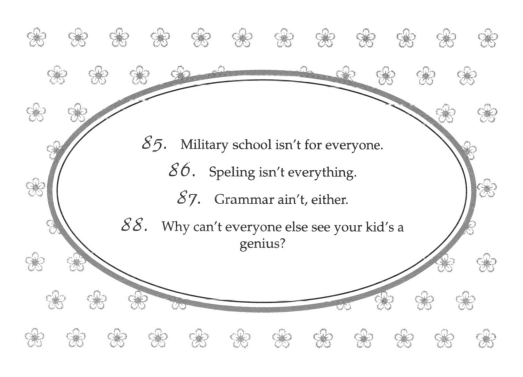

85. Military school isn't for everyone.

86. Speling isn't everything.

87. Grammar ain't, either.

88. Why can't everyone else see your kid's a genius?

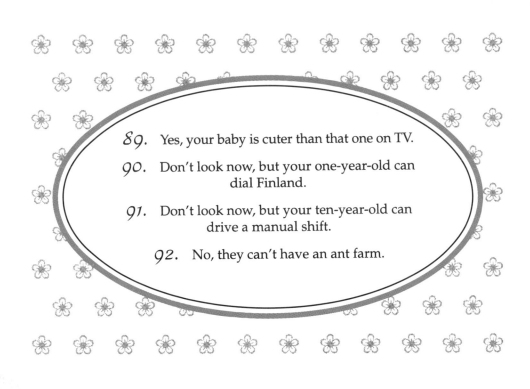

89. Yes, your baby is cuter than that one on TV.

90. Don't look now, but your one-year-old can dial Finland.

91. Don't look now, but your ten-year-old can drive a manual shift.

92. No, they can't have an ant farm.

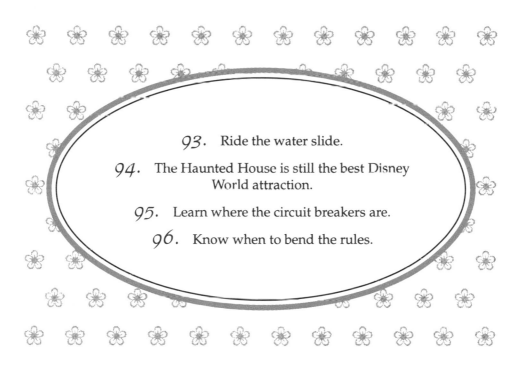

93. Ride the water slide.

94. The Haunted House is still the best Disney World attraction.

95. Learn where the circuit breakers are.

96. Know when to bend the rules.

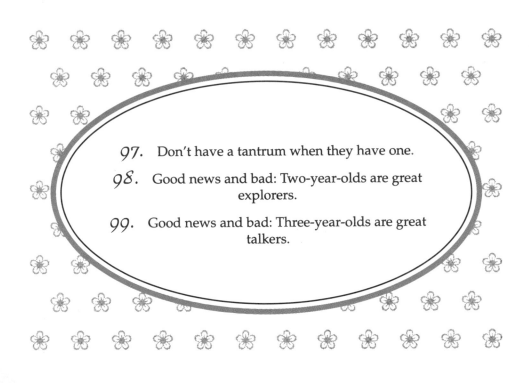

97. Don't have a tantrum when they have one.

98. Good news and bad: Two-year-olds are great explorers.

99. Good news and bad: Three-year-olds are great talkers.

100. Good news and bad: Four-year-olds are great finger-painters.

101. Don't put toast points in your son's lunchbox.

102. Jump in the leaves with them.

103. Learn to make a good pot of chili.

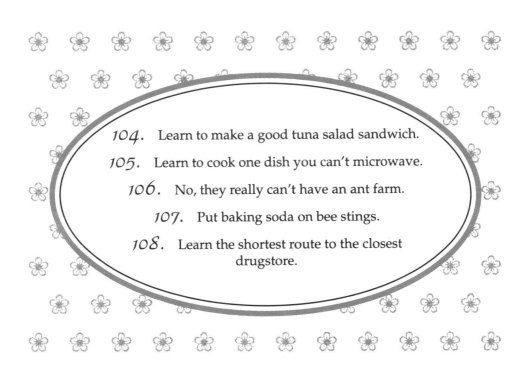

104. Learn to make a good tuna salad sandwich.

105. Learn to cook one dish you can't microwave.

106. No, they really can't have an ant farm.

107. Put baking soda on bee stings.

108. Learn the shortest route to the closest drugstore.

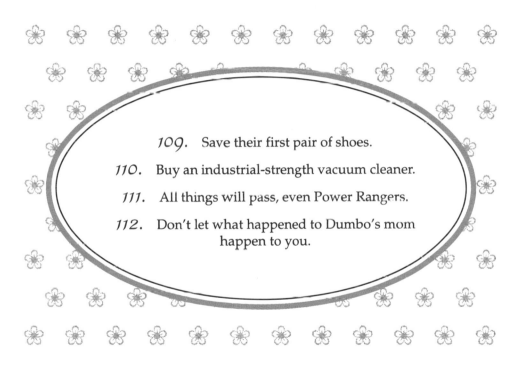

109. Save their first pair of shoes.

110. Buy an industrial-strength vacuum cleaner.

111. All things will pass, even Power Rangers.

112. Don't let what happened to Dumbo's mom happen to you.

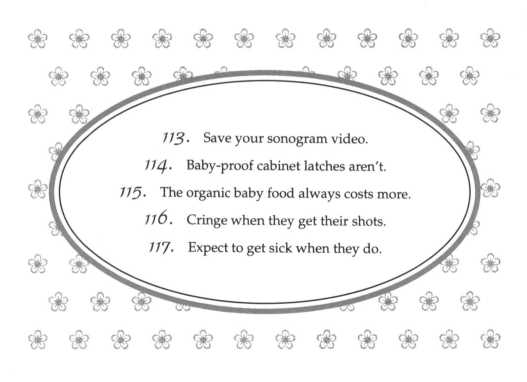

113. Save your sonogram video.

114. Baby-proof cabinet latches aren't.

115. The organic baby food always costs more.

116. Cringe when they get their shots.

117. Expect to get sick when they do.

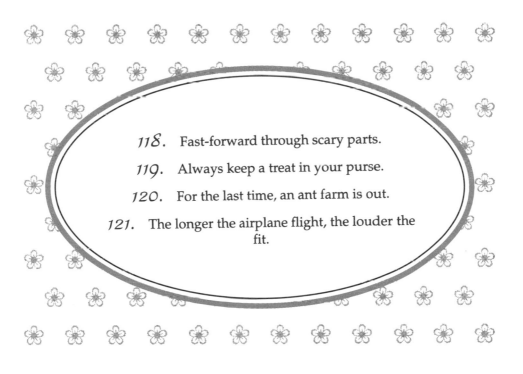

118. Fast-forward through scary parts.

119. Always keep a treat in your purse.

120. For the last time, an ant farm is out.

121. The longer the airplane flight, the louder the fit.

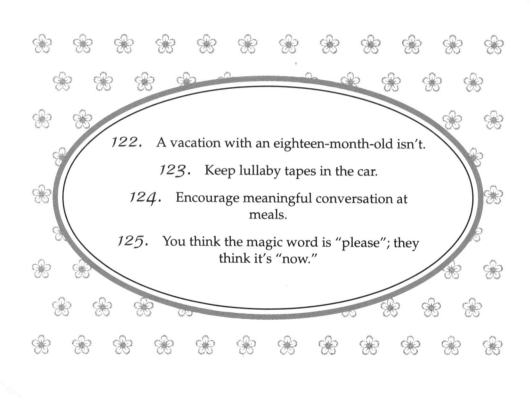

122. A vacation with an eighteen-month-old isn't.

123. Keep lullaby tapes in the car.

124. Encourage meaningful conversation at meals.

125. You think the magic word is "please"; they think it's "now."

126. Accept your limitations.

127. Make the most of your talents.

128. Join in with their play fantasies.

129. If you can't do it while they're napping, you can't do it at all.

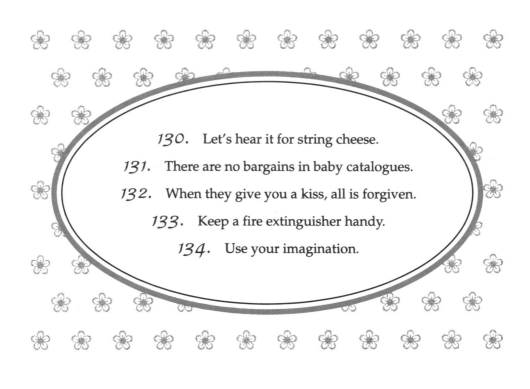

130. Let's hear it for string cheese.

131. There are no bargains in baby catalogues.

132. When they give you a kiss, all is forgiven.

133. Keep a fire extinguisher handy.

134. Use your imagination.

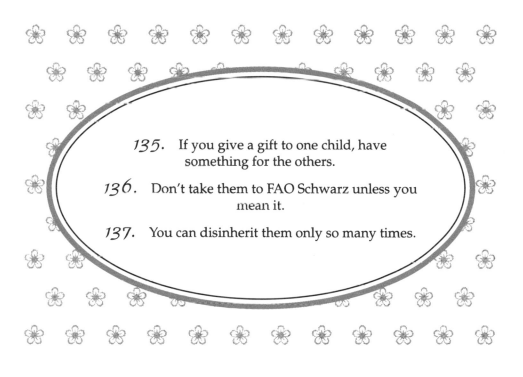

135. If you give a gift to one child, have something for the others.

136. Don't take them to FAO Schwarz unless you mean it.

137. You can disinherit them only so many times.

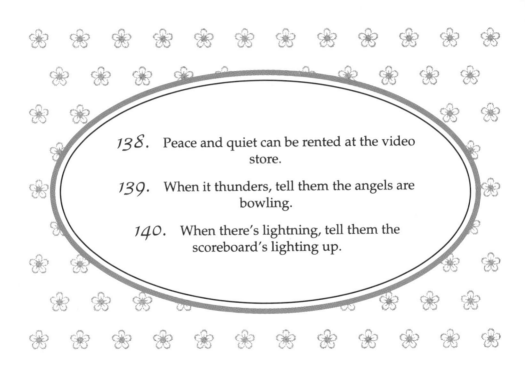

138. Peace and quiet can be rented at the video store.

139. When it thunders, tell them the angels are bowling.

140. When there's lightning, tell them the scoreboard's lighting up.

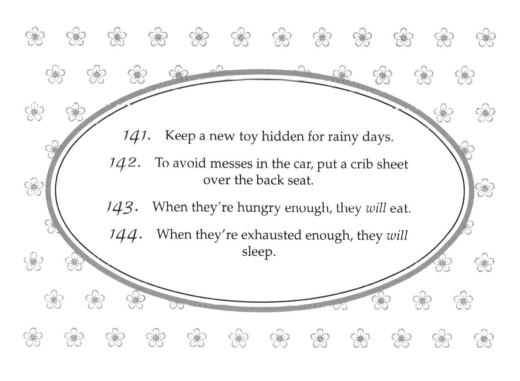

141. Keep a new toy hidden for rainy days.

142. To avoid messes in the car, put a crib sheet over the back seat.

143. When they're hungry enough, they *will* eat.

144. When they're exhausted enough, they *will* sleep.

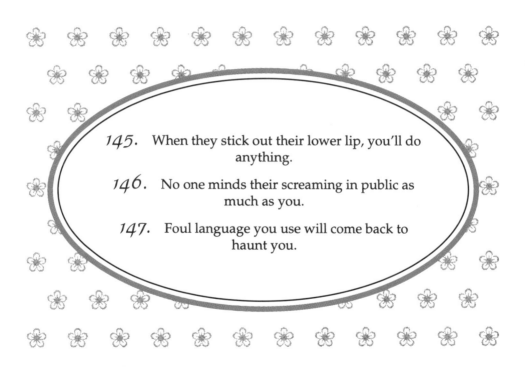

145. When they stick out their lower lip, you'll do anything.

146. No one minds their screaming in public as much as you.

147. Foul language you use will come back to haunt you.

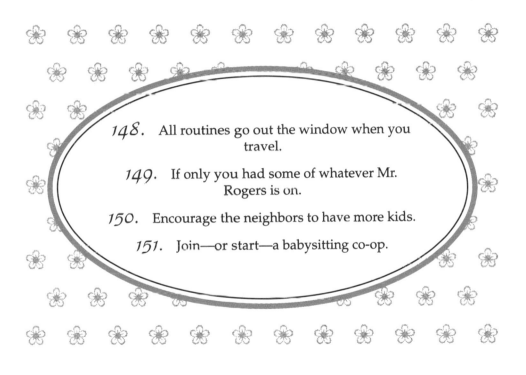

148. All routines go out the window when you travel.

149. If only you had some of whatever Mr. Rogers is on.

150. Encourage the neighbors to have more kids.

151. Join—or start—a babysitting co-op.

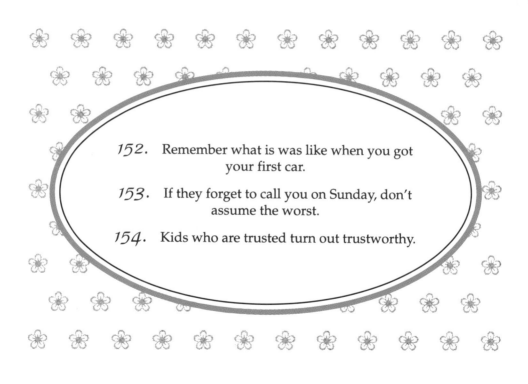

152. Remember what is was like when you got your first car.

153. If they forget to call you on Sunday, don't assume the worst.

154. Kids who are trusted turn out trustworthy.

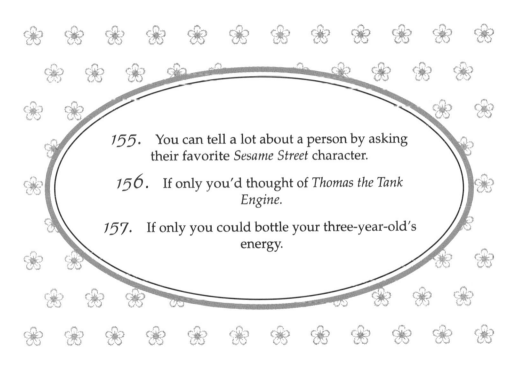

155. You can tell a lot about a person by asking their favorite *Sesame Street* character.

156. If only you'd thought of *Thomas the Tank Engine*.

157. If only you could bottle your three-year-old's energy.

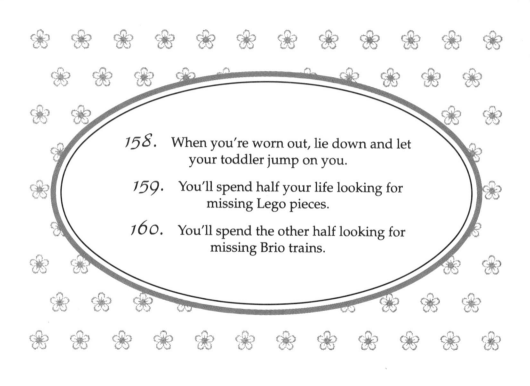

158. When you're worn out, lie down and let your toddler jump on you.

159. You'll spend half your life looking for missing Lego pieces.

160. You'll spend the other half looking for missing Brio trains.

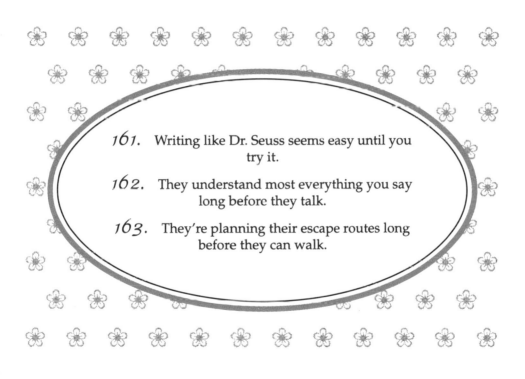

161. Writing like Dr. Seuss seems easy until you try it.

162. They understand most everything you say long before they talk.

163. They're planning their escape routes long before they can walk.

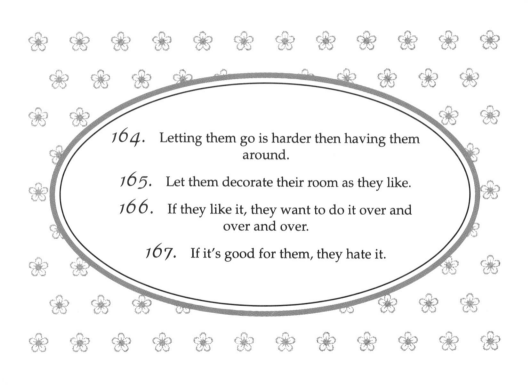

164. Letting them go is harder then having them around.

165. Let them decorate their room as they like.

166. If they like it, they want to do it over and over and over.

167. If it's good for them, they hate it.

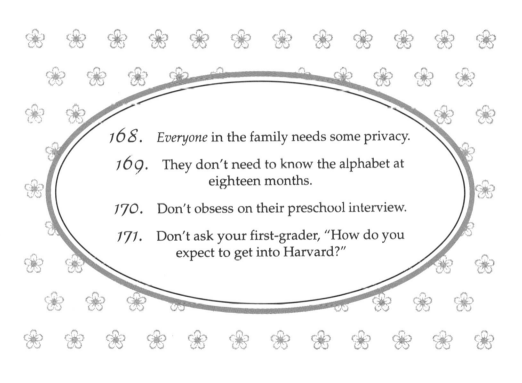

168. *Everyone* in the family needs some privacy.

169. They don't need to know the alphabet at eighteen months.

170. Don't obsess on their preschool interview.

171. Don't ask your first-grader, "How do you expect to get into Harvard?"

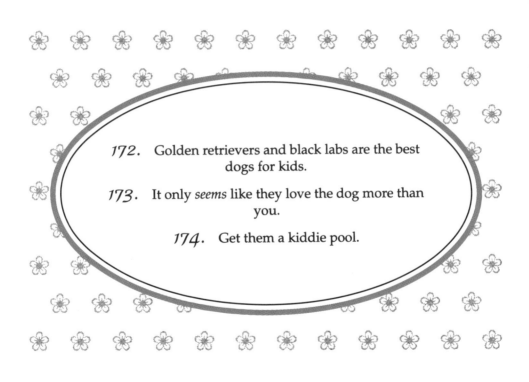

172. Golden retrievers and black labs are the best dogs for kids.

173. It only *seems* like they love the dog more than you.

174. Get them a kiddie pool.

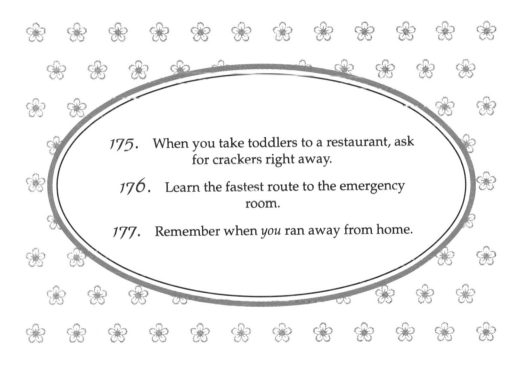

175. When you take toddlers to a restaurant, ask for crackers right away.

176. Learn the fastest route to the emergency room.

177. Remember when *you* ran away from home.

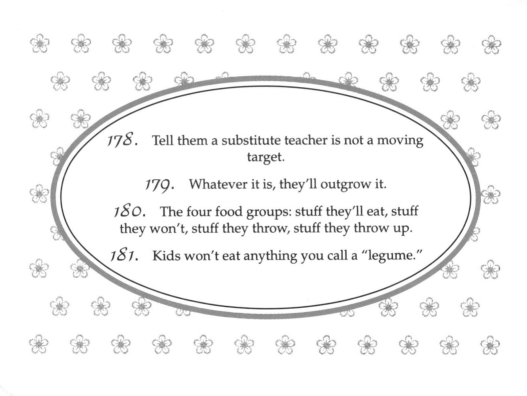

178. Tell them a substitute teacher is not a moving target.

179. Whatever it is, they'll outgrow it.

180. The four food groups: stuff they'll eat, stuff they won't, stuff they throw, stuff they throw up.

181. Kids won't eat anything you call a "legume."

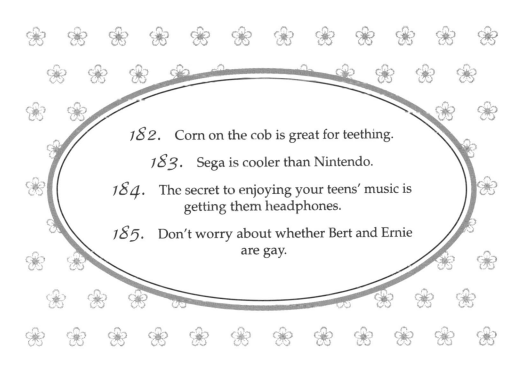

182. Corn on the cob is great for teething.

183. Sega is cooler than Nintendo.

184. The secret to enjoying your teens' music is getting them headphones.

185. Don't worry about whether Bert and Ernie are gay.

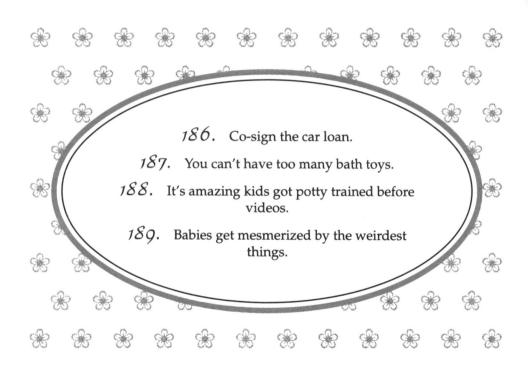

186. Co-sign the car loan.

187. You can't have too many bath toys.

188. It's amazing kids got potty trained before videos.

189. Babies get mesmerized by the weirdest things.

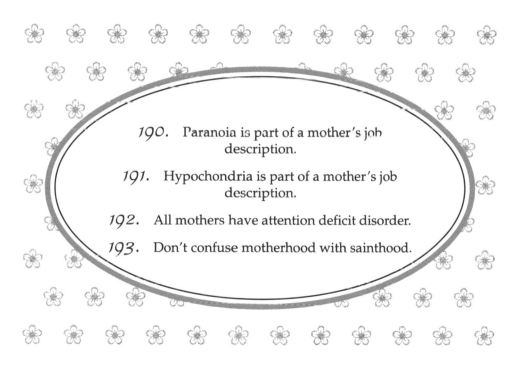

190. Paranoia is part of a mother's job description.

191. Hypochondria is part of a mother's job description.

192. All mothers have attention deficit disorder.

193. Don't confuse motherhood with sainthood.

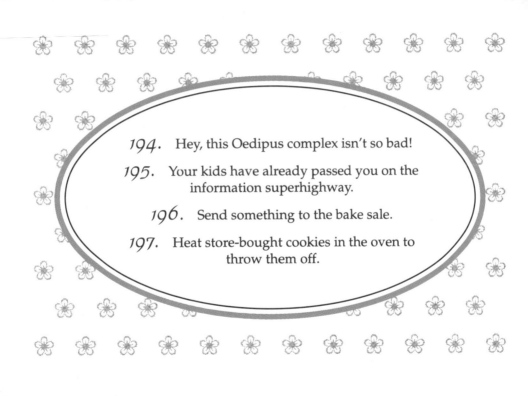

194. Hey, this Oedipus complex isn't so bad!

195. Your kids have already passed you on the information superhighway.

196. Send something to the bake sale.

197. Heat store-bought cookies in the oven to throw them off.

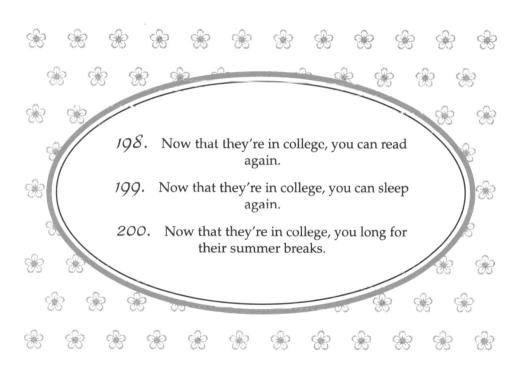

198. Now that they're in college, you can read again.

199. Now that they're in college, you can sleep again.

200. Now that they're in college, you long for their summer breaks.

201. Send them back to the dorm with a pan of your homemade lasagna.

202. Hope the ozone layer comes back when they grow up.

203. Hope they won't be the ones to colonize Mars.

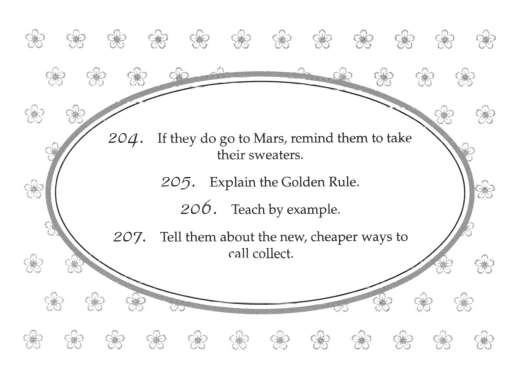

204. If they do go to Mars, remind them to take their sweaters.

205. Explain the Golden Rule.

206. Teach by example.

207. Tell them about the new, cheaper ways to call collect.

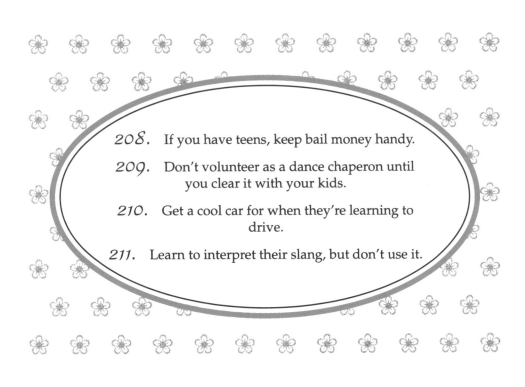

208. If you have teens, keep bail money handy.

209. Don't volunteer as a dance chaperon until you clear it with your kids.

210. Get a cool car for when they're learning to drive.

211. Learn to interpret their slang, but don't use it.

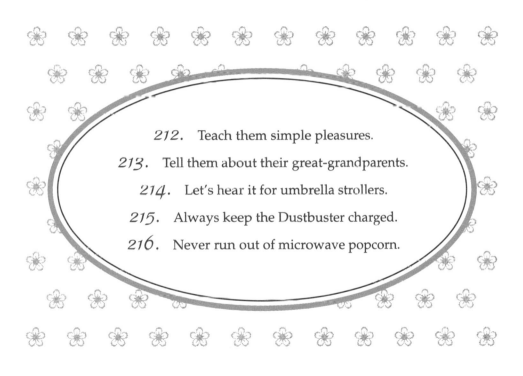

212. Teach them simple pleasures.

213. Tell them about their great-grandparents.

214. Let's hear it for umbrella strollers.

215. Always keep the Dustbuster charged.

216. Never run out of microwave popcorn.

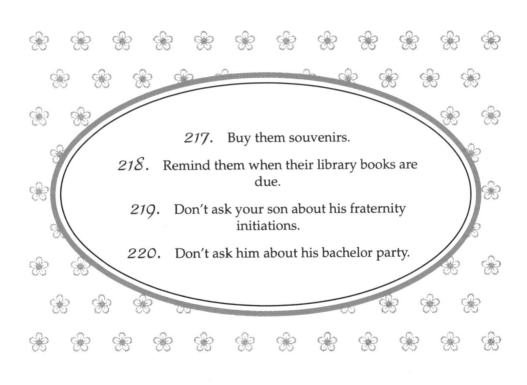

217. Buy them souvenirs.

218. Remind them when their library books are due.

219. Don't ask your son about his fraternity initiations.

220. Don't ask him about his bachelor party.

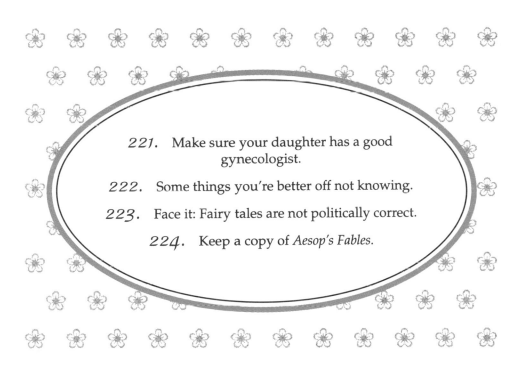

221. Make sure your daughter has a good gynecologist.

222. Some things you're better off not knowing.

223. Face it: Fairy tales are not politically correct.

224. Keep a copy of *Aesop's Fables*.

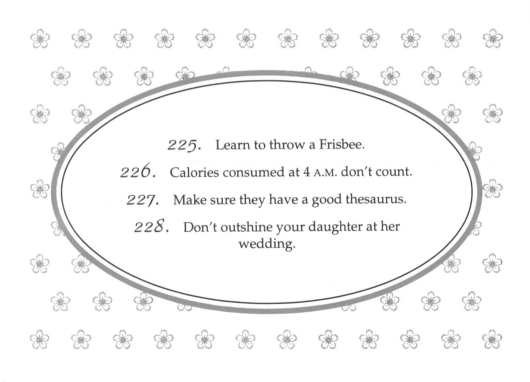

225. Learn to throw a Frisbee.

226. Calories consumed at 4 A.M. don't count.

227. Make sure they have a good thesaurus.

228. Don't outshine your daughter at her wedding.

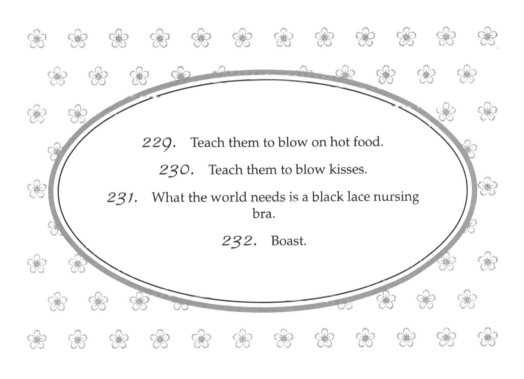

229. Teach them to blow on hot food.

230. Teach them to blow kisses.

231. What the world needs is a black lace nursing bra.

232. Boast.

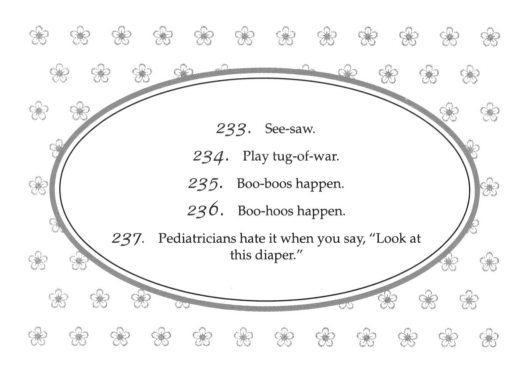

233. See-saw.

234. Play tug-of-war.

235. Boo-boos happen.

236. Boo-hoos happen.

237. Pediatricians hate it when you say, "Look at this diaper."

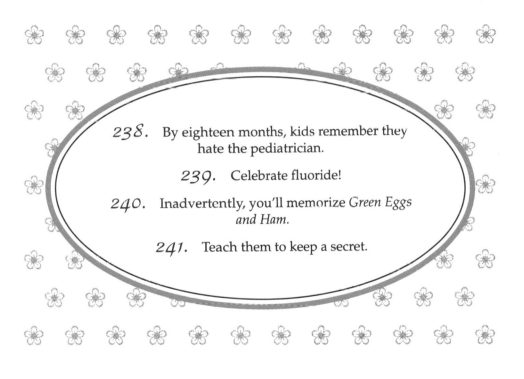

238. By eighteen months, kids remember they hate the pediatrician.

239. Celebrate fluoride!

240. Inadvertently, you'll memorize *Green Eggs and Ham*.

241. Teach them to keep a secret.

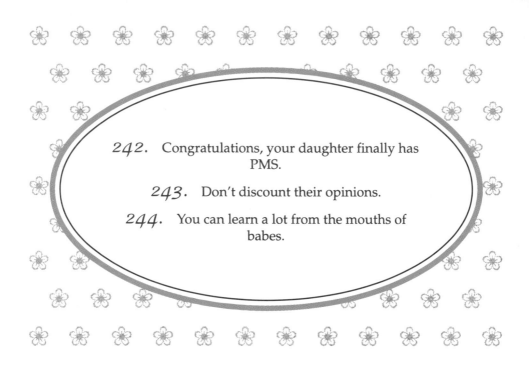

242. Congratulations, your daughter finally has PMS.

243. Don't discount their opinions.

244. You can learn a lot from the mouths of babes.

245. "Because I'm your mother" is a perfectly good reason.

246. Whenever they sprain something, Dad's at the office.

247. Whenever they break something, Dad's out of town.

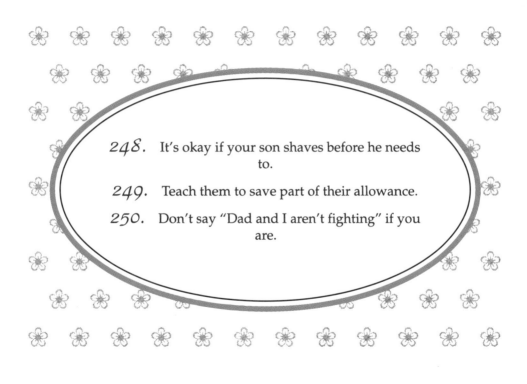

248. It's okay if your son shaves before he needs to.

249. Teach them to save part of their allowance.

250. Don't say "Dad and I aren't fighting" if you are.

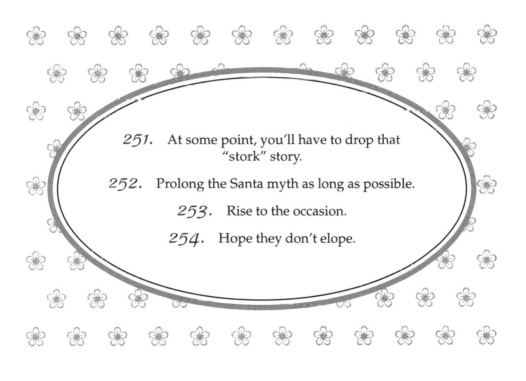

251. At some point, you'll have to drop that "stork" story.

252. Prolong the Santa myth as long as possible.

253. Rise to the occasion.

254. Hope they don't elope.

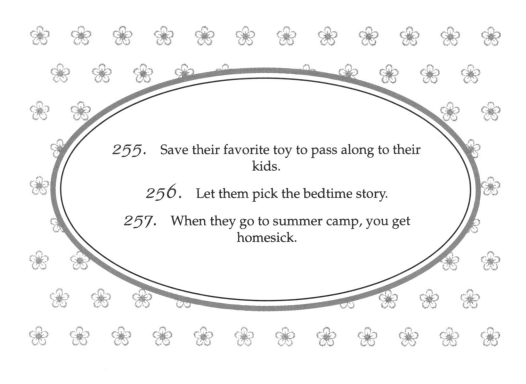

255. Save their favorite toy to pass along to their kids.

256. Let them pick the bedtime story.

257. When they go to summer camp, you get homesick.

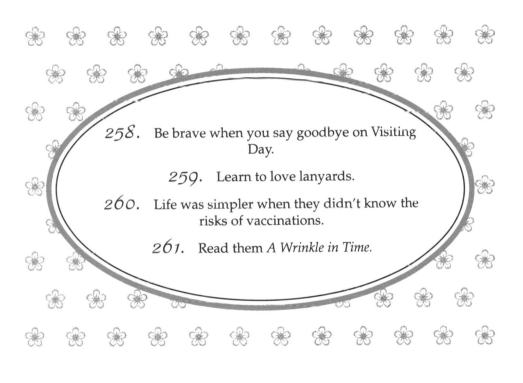

258. Be brave when you say goodbye on Visiting Day.

259. Learn to love lanyards.

260. Life was simpler when they didn't know the risks of vaccinations.

261. Read them *A Wrinkle in Time.*

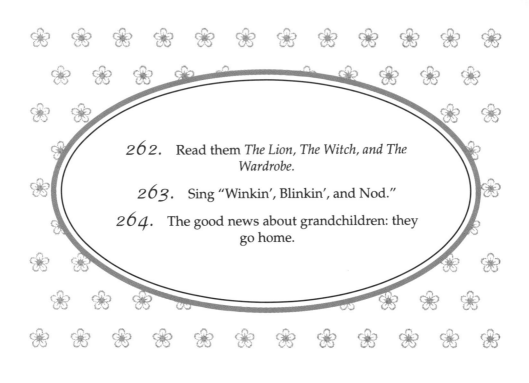

262. Read them *The Lion, The Witch, and The Wardrobe.*

263. Sing "Winkin', Blinkin', and Nod."

264. The good news about grandchildren: they go home.

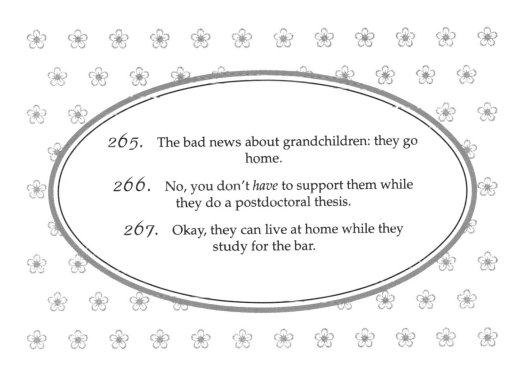

265. The bad news about grandchildren: they go home.

266. No, you don't *have* to support them while they do a postdoctoral thesis.

267. Okay, they can live at home while they study for the bar.

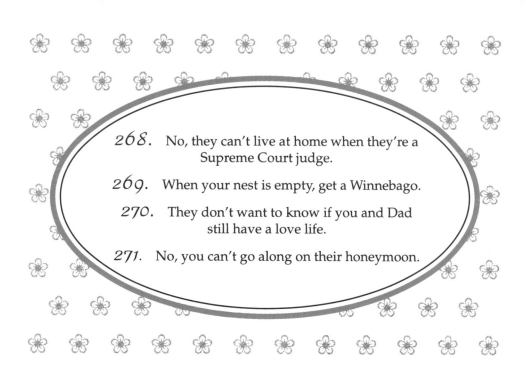

268. No, they can't live at home when they're a Supreme Court judge.

269. When your nest is empty, get a Winnebago.

270. They don't want to know if you and Dad still have a love life.

271. No, you can't go along on their honeymoon.

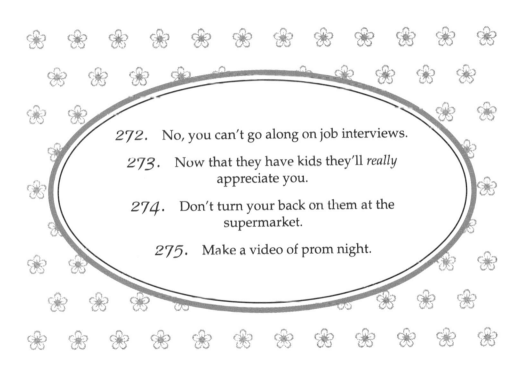

272. No, you can't go along on job interviews.

273. Now that they have kids they'll *really* appreciate you.

274. Don't turn your back on them at the supermarket.

275. Make a video of prom night.

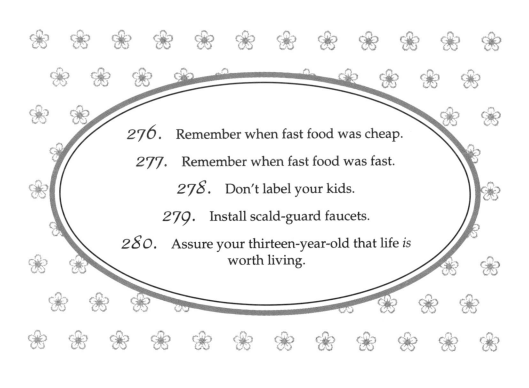

276. Remember when fast food was cheap.

277. Remember when fast food was fast.

278. Don't label your kids.

279. Install scald-guard faucets.

280. Assure your thirteen-year-old that life *is* worth living.

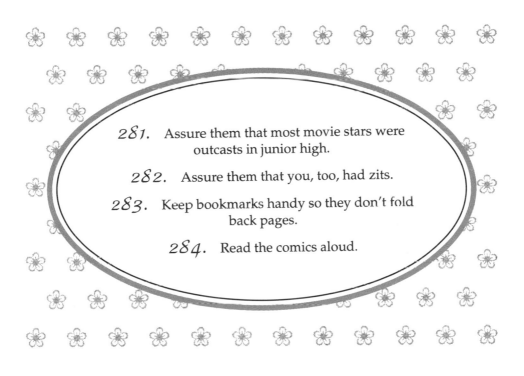

281. Assure them that most movie stars were outcasts in junior high.

282. Assure them that you, too, had zits.

283. Keep bookmarks handy so they don't fold back pages.

284. Read the comics aloud.

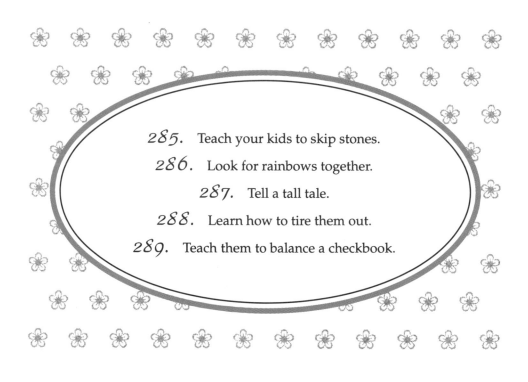

285. Teach your kids to skip stones.

286. Look for rainbows together.

287. Tell a tall tale.

288. Learn how to tire them out.

289. Teach them to balance a checkbook.

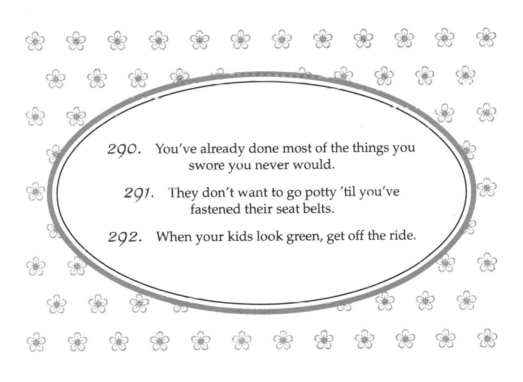

290. You've already done most of the things you swore you never would.

291. They don't want to go potty 'til you've fastened their seat belts.

292. When your kids look green, get off the ride.

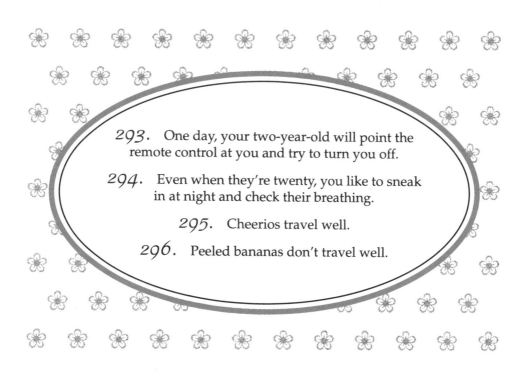

293. One day, your two-year-old will point the remote control at you and try to turn you off.

294. Even when they're twenty, you like to sneak in at night and check their breathing.

295. Cheerios travel well.

296. Peeled bananas don't travel well.

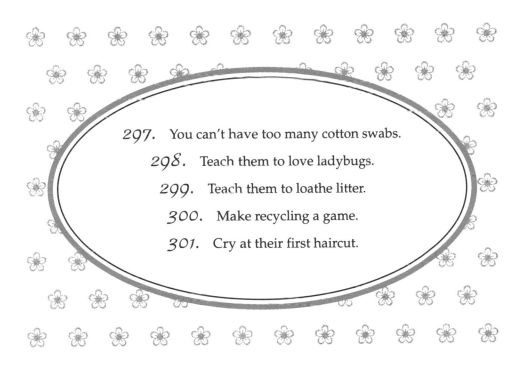

297. You can't have too many cotton swabs.

298. Teach them to love ladybugs.

299. Teach them to loathe litter.

300. Make recycling a game.

301. Cry at their first haircut.

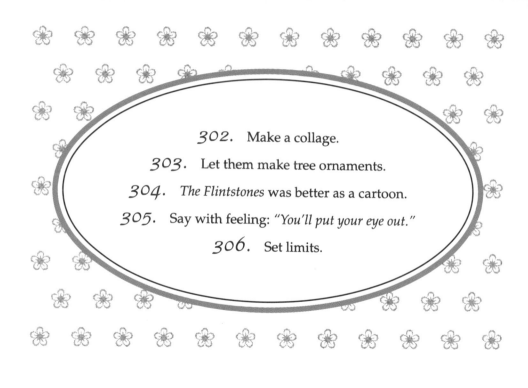

302. Make a collage.

303. Let them make tree ornaments.

304. *The Flintstones* was better as a cartoon.

305. Say with feeling: *"You'll put your eye out."*

306. Set limits.

307. Roll with the punches.

308. No, they can't have a chain saw.

309. Make an indoor picnic on a rainy day.

310. You can't see *E.T.* too many times.

311. Their school cafeteria smells just like yours did.

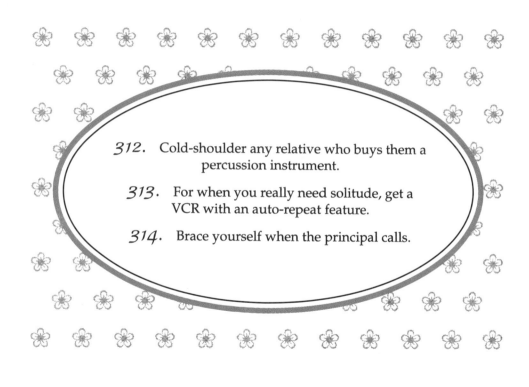

312. Cold-shoulder any relative who buys them a
percussion instrument.

313. For when you really need solitude, get a
VCR with an auto-repeat feature.

314. Brace yourself when the principal calls.

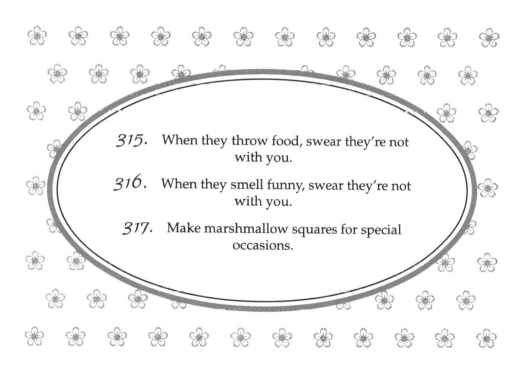

315. When they throw food, swear they're not with you.

316. When they smell funny, swear they're not with you.

317. Make marshmallow squares for special occasions.

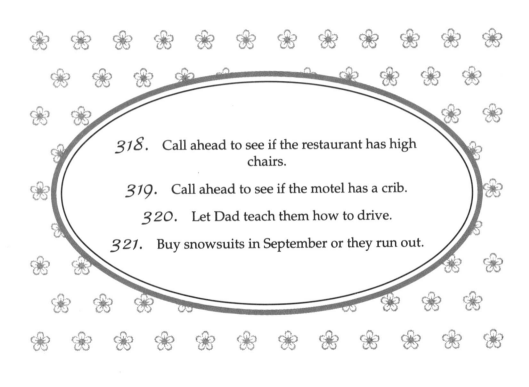

318. Call ahead to see if the restaurant has high chairs.

319. Call ahead to see if the motel has a crib.

320. Let Dad teach them how to drive.

321. Buy snowsuits in September or they run out.

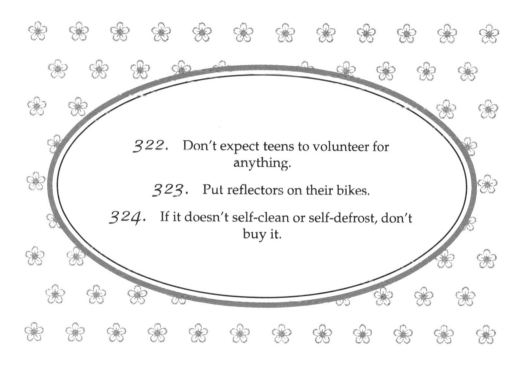

322. Don't expect teens to volunteer for anything.

323. Put reflectors on their bikes.

324. If it doesn't self-clean or self-defrost, don't buy it.

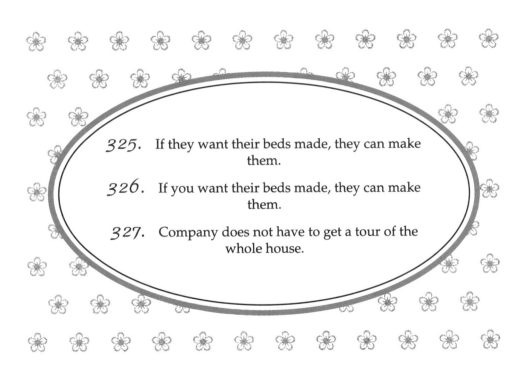

325. If they want their beds made, they can make them.

326. If you want their beds made, they can make them.

327. Company does not have to get a tour of the whole house.

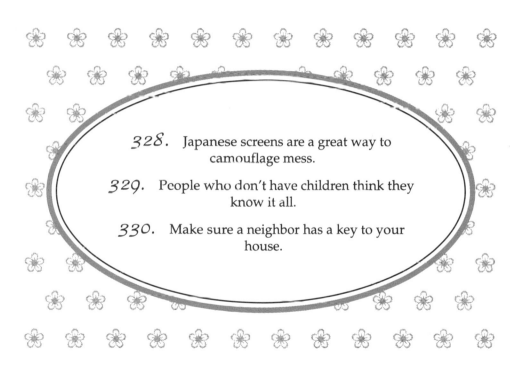

328. Japanese screens are a great way to camouflage mess.

329. People who don't have children think they know it all.

330. Make sure a neighbor has a key to your house.

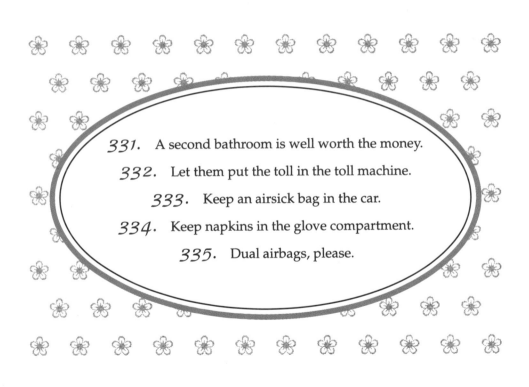

331. A second bathroom is well worth the money.

332. Let them put the toll in the toll machine.

333. Keep an airsick bag in the car.

334. Keep napkins in the glove compartment.

335. Dual airbags, please.

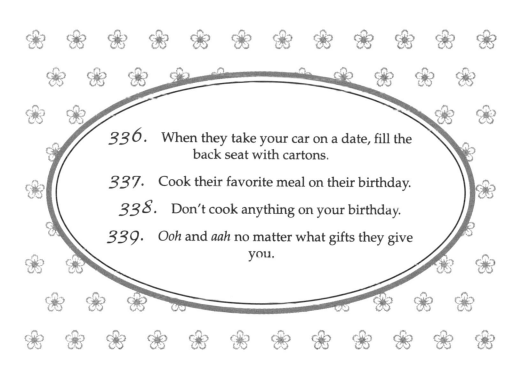

336. When they take your car on a date, fill the back seat with cartons.

337. Cook their favorite meal on their birthday.

338. Don't cook anything on your birthday.

339. *Ooh* and *aah* no matter what gifts they give you.

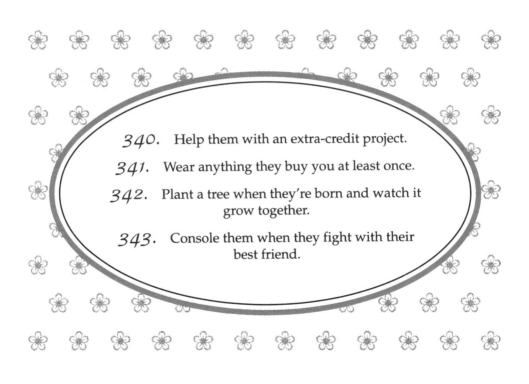

340. Help them with an extra-credit project.

341. Wear anything they buy you at least once.

342. Plant a tree when they're born and watch it grow together.

343. Console them when they fight with their best friend.

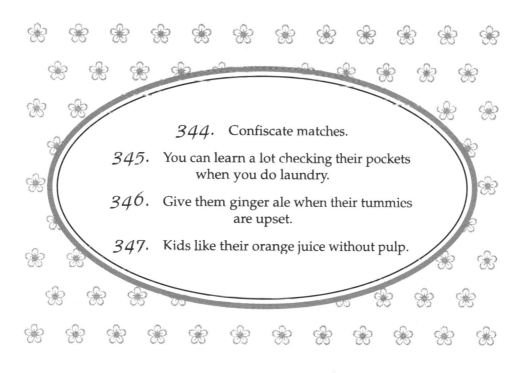

344. Confiscate matches.

345. You can learn a lot checking their pockets when you do laundry.

346. Give them ginger ale when their tummies are upset.

347. Kids like their orange juice without pulp.

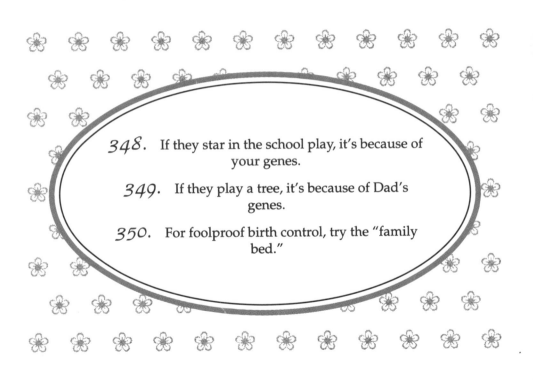

348. If they star in the school play, it's because of your genes.

349. If they play a tree, it's because of Dad's genes.

350. For foolproof birth control, try the "family bed."

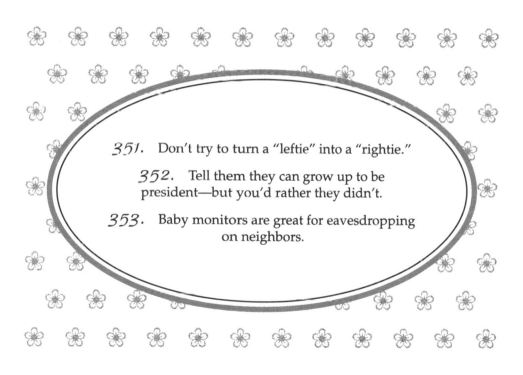

351. Don't try to turn a "leftie" into a "rightie."

352. Tell them they can grow up to be president—but you'd rather they didn't.

353. Baby monitors are great for eavesdropping on neighbors.

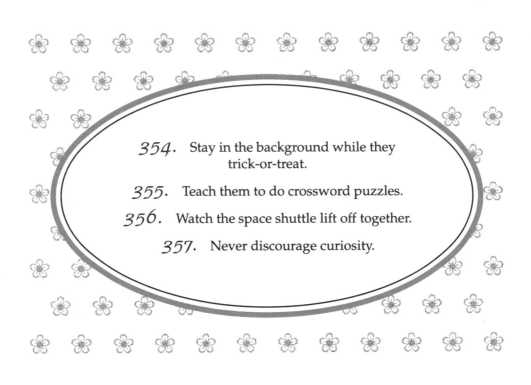

354. Stay in the background while they trick-or-treat.

355. Teach them to do crossword puzzles.

356. Watch the space shuttle lift off together.

357. Never discourage curiosity.

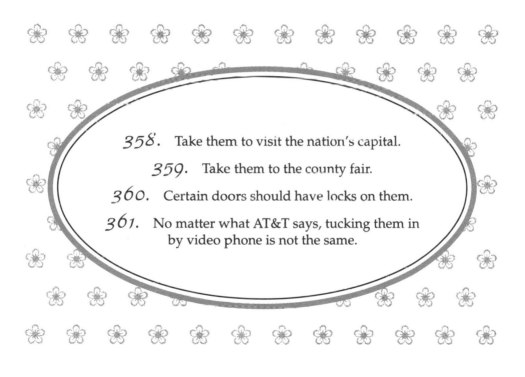

358. Take them to visit the nation's capital.

359. Take them to the county fair.

360. Certain doors should have locks on them.

361. No matter what AT&T says, tucking them in by video phone is not the same.

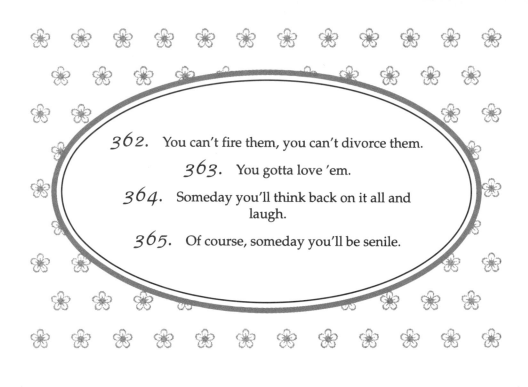

362. You can't fire them, you can't divorce them.

363. You gotta love 'em.

364. Someday you'll think back on it all and laugh.

365. Of course, someday you'll be senile.